IMAGES IN PROCESSION

TESTIMONIES TO SPANISH FAITH

By Patrick Lenaghan

AMERICAN BIBLE SOCIETY   THE HISPANIC SOCIETY OF AMERICA

New York, 2000

Exhibition dates at the Gallery at the American Bible Society:
February 3 – April 29, 2000

The exhibition is a collaboration between the American Bible Society and The Hispanic Society of America.

Text: Copyright © 2000, American Bible Society and The Hispanic Society of America
Anderson Photographs: Copyright © 2000, The Hispanic Society of America

ISBN 1-585161101

The exhibition was curated by Dr. Patrick Lenaghan, Curator at The Hispanic Society of America, and organized at the American Bible Society by Dr. Ena Heller, Director of the Gallery.

Catalogue published by the American Bible Society and The Hispanic Society of America.

Exhibition prints made from the original Anderson negatives by Roberto Sandoval for The Hispanic Society of America.

Catalogue and graphic design: Gary Skeggs, Skeggs Design, New York, NY
Exhibition design: Lou Storey, Red Bank, NJ

Printed in the United States.

Table of Contents

American Bible Society President's Preface	IV
The Hispanic Society of America President's Preface	VI
Map of Spain	VIII
Introduction	IX
Chapter 1: Spanish Religious Processions: Holy Week and Corpus Christi	1
Chapter 2: Art and Processions in Spain and the New World	15
Chapter 3: Ruth Anderson: Photographer of Spanish Life and Customs in the 1920s	31
Anderson Photographs and Commentary	41
Zamora: Good Friday, April 2, 1926	42
Villalcampo: Easter Monday, April 5, 1926	52
Jerez de los Caballeros: Palm Sunday, April 1, 1928; Maundy Thursday, April 5, 1928; and Good Friday, April 6, 1928	64
La Alberca: Assumption of the Virgin, August 15-17, 1930	86
Checklist	108
Notes	110
Bibliography	115

President's Preface

THE AMERICAN BIBLE SOCIETY IS PLEASED TO PRESENT *Images in Procession: Testimonies to Spanish Faith*, an exhibition in collaboration with The Hispanic Society of America. This exhibition explores the Spanish tradition of religious celebrations in which representations of Jesus, Mary and other Biblical figures are carried in processions, a tradition with deep roots that is still practiced today.

As an organization committed to spreading the Holy Scripture, we are happy to present an exhibition exploring the historically rich tradition of Christian art and culture in Spain and Latin America. The project began with a selection of photographs from The Hispanic Society's collection, many of which had never been exhibited, but soon grew to include sculpture and painting that reflect the symbolism, spirituality, and emotionalism of these rituals. We are grateful to The Hispanic Society of America for providing us the photographs, paintings and sculpture that comprise most of the show and to Dr. Patrick Lenaghan, Curator of Prints and Photographs, who curated the exhibition and wrote the catalogue. Without his expertise the show could not have been realized.

Our gratitude goes to the museums whose loans greatly enriched our show: the Denver Museum of Art; the Martin D'Arcy Gallery of Art, Loyola University Museum; and the Yale University Art Museum.

Finally, we thank the many individuals who helped make the show a reality. This exhibition would have been unthinkable without the generous support of the Board of Trustees of the American Bible Society. The Director of the Gallery, Dr. Ena Heller, organized the logistics of securing the various loans and the funding which made the exhibition, catalogue, and educational programs possible. Patricia Pongracz, Exhibition Coordinator, oversaw the shipping and installation of the objects, and kept the schedule for the myriad production steps of the catalogue and printed materials. Dr. Liana Lupas, Curator of the Scripture Collection, curated a complementary exhibition from the Library's extensive holdings. In this project, she received significant support from

Mary Jane Ballou, Director of the Library and Archives. Dorothea Colligan, Preservation Specialist, ensured the stability of the books in their display. Mildred Mas and Alain Sasson, Production Department, shepherded the catalogue through printing. In the Department of Communications, Bob Briggs, David Singer, Linda Langergaard, and Dulce Alvarado provided invaluable support for in-house design and administration. James Walker oversaw the production of the video now seen in the Education Center. Kristen Robitaille, Graduate Student Intern at the Gallery, oversaw many administrative details, and worked closely in the development of the children's education program.

Lou Storey, Lou Storey Exhibition Design, envisioned the exhibition from concept through installation. His thoughtful understanding of the art and the missions of the American Bible Society and The Hispanic Society of America resulted in a display pleasing to all. Gary Skeggs, Skeggs Design, created the graphic identity for the exhibition. The installation was facilitated by Michael Mikulay; Craig Oleszewski of Art Preservation Services; and building engineering and maintenance staff: Paul Mehl, Bob Maynes, Aurel Macovei, Kevin Bonner, Odilon Arriga, Olmedo Gavaria, and Paul Perez.

Dr. Eugene Habecker
President of the American Bible Society

President's Preface

At the Hispanic Society of America, we are delighted to have collaborated with the American Bible Society on *Images in Procession: Testimonies of Spanish Faith*. This exhibition examines a religious practice common in Spain but unfamiliar to many North Americans: processions of religious statues. The project began with the Hispanic Society's collection of photographs taken in the 1920s by Ruth Anderson, a Hispanic Society curator and photographer, many of which had never been exhibited before. Soon the project grew to include reliefs, statues, and paintings that reflect the art at the center of these rituals. The commitment of the Gallery at the American Bible Society to exhibitions that foster appreciation of Judeo-Christian Art has made that institution an ideal partner for this project. For the Hispanic Society, this exhibition affords an opportunity to advance the appreciation of Spanish art and culture, the purpose for which the institution was founded in 1904 by Archer M. Huntington. Moreover, because this project demonstrates the relevance of artistic expression in the daily life of Spain, it offers a notable opportunity to continue Huntington's vision of a museum dedicated to the many facets of that country's cultural heritage.

We at the Hispanic Society take great pleasure in acknowledging the active participation of the Bible Society in every phase of the exhibition. Dr. Ena Heller, Gallery Director, and Patricia Pongracz, Exhibitions Coordinator, provided invaluable advice and suggestions from the definition of the project to the final design, all of which have strengthened it significantly. The designers contracted by the Bible Society, Lou Storey for installation design and Gary Skeggs for catalogue and graphic design, played a key role by shaping and refining the presentation of the exhibition both in the gallery and in print. Moreover, their work has helped us to see our objects in a new light.

We are also pleased to recognize the contributions of several people outside of the Bible Society and the Hispanic Society who have contributed towards the research and preparation of the catalogue. Dr. Carrie Hamilton read numerous drafts, and her suggestions improved them significantly. In Spain, the photographer Cristina García Rodero shared her experiences of Spanish popular festivals and, in the process, enhanced the appreciation of Anderson's accomplishments as a photographer. The town hall of Jerez de los Caballeros was particularly forthcoming with information regarding current celebrations of Holy Week there. In the United States, important object conservation was provided by The Textile Conservation Workshop where a team led by Muffie Austin directed treatment of the statue of Virgin (The Hispanic Society of America, LD520).

The staff at the Hispanic Society has also played a vital role in this project. Dr. Patrick Lenaghan, Curator of Prints and Photographs, not only proposed the initial idea but has also curated the exhibition and written the catalogue. Throughout, he has been expertly aided by Mencía Figueroa Villota, Research Assistant in the Department of Prints and Photographs. Roberto Sandoval, Photography Department, worked with great skill developing the exhibition prints from Anderson's original negatives, which was frequently a challenging task given the low density of their emulsion. Belén Alvarez Pro, Conservation Department, restored several statues for the exhibition, most notably the eighteenth-century polychromed figure of St. Joseph. Dr. John O'Neill, Curator of Rare Books, edited the catalogue with characteristic attention to detail. Both Dr. Marcus Burke, Curator of Paintings, and Dr. Mitchell Codding, Director, have generously shared their expertise on Colonial Latin American Art and Culture and actively supported the project. William N. Ambler, Public Affairs Coordinator, and Camilla Olaso, Friends Group, oversaw press releases and, more broadly, public outreach from the Hispanic Society.

Dr. Theodore S. Beardsley Jr.
President of The Hispanic Society of America

Map of Spain drawn by Ruth Anderson for her book *Costumes Painted by Sorolla in His Provinces of Spain*. 1957.

INTRODUCTION

WHILE STAYING AT THE HOTEL SUIZO IN ZAMORA, Ruth Anderson "was awakened by hurrying footsteps on the pavement" at 4:30 in the morning of April 2, 1926. She "went to the window and saw *penitentes* in black carrying black wooden crosses in the dark street." It was Good Friday, and she was witnessing the first of the religious processions held that day in observance of Christ's Passion. Here, as in all Spain, local citizens took statues, some dating from the seventeenth century, out of their churches and carried them throughout the city in elaborate ceremonies. Accompanying these images were *penitentes*, hooded figures wearing conical hats, who marched carrying a cross and *nazarenos*, similarly clad figures, who walked silently to atone for their sins. These rites occurred as part of the city's celebration of Holy Week, the week beginning with Palm Sunday and ending with Easter Sunday. For Christians, this week which commemorates Christ's suffering, death, and resurrection comprises the most solemn moment of the liturgical calendar, and the Spanish mark it each year with a series of processions like those in Zamora on Good Friday 1926.

Ruth Anderson had traveled to Spain to photograph such customs as part of a program to document Spanish life for The Hispanic Society of America, the museum where she worked as a curator and photographer. Thus April 2 found her in Zamora. The photographs she took that day and those of comparable processions which she made on other trips during the 1920s vividly evoke these rites. The images she captured offer an opportunity to study the Spanish tradition of religious celebrations with processions of statues, observances which have deep roots in their communities and yet continue to this day. Because they are linked to beliefs tenaciously embedded in Spanish culture, these rites require a careful evaluation of the faith and society which created them and whose needs they address. Consequently, essays on the history of these processions and the art borne out on these days precede a discussion of the photographs.

Many visitors to Spain have found these processions puzzling and strange. In part, their response results from different assumptions about religious practices and decorum, a divergence with deep historical roots. When the Reformation separated Christianity into Catholics and Protestants in the sixteenth century, the role of ritual provoked heated polemics. The Catholic Church continued to foster many disputed rites as well as the emotions they released whereas Protestants remained distrustful of these practices. Correspondingly, such processions seem unsettling to many non-Catholic visitors. Even within the Catholic world, the Spanish celebrations are distinctive for the extent to which they involve entire communities, including secular authorities, and the impassioned response they elicit. To most foreigners, the veneration accorded the statues at these moments verges on worship of the image itself and not the God or saints depicted. Further, the overt emotionalism and sensual impact of these ceremonies trouble those raised in a more austere faith. Nonetheless, it is hoped that by examining the history of religious processions and their artistic expression, this exhibition will elucidate these rites as demonstrations of an emotional world view which blends religious and social considerations almost seamlessly.

CHAPTER 1

SPANISH PROCESSIONS: HOLY WEEK AND CORPUS CHRISTI

THE PRACTICE OF CARRYING OUT RELIGIOUS STATUES had been widespread throughout the Middle Ages and Early Modern Era and can still be found in other parts of Catholic Europe today. Nonetheless, the extent to which these rituals continue in Spain, particularly during Holy Week, is exceptional. Although the processions of Holy Week occupy a special place in their religious calendar, Spaniards also hold such events on other major feasts: Corpus Christi, the Assumption, and those of local saints. The study of these rites thus presents a broad undertaking. To begin, the structure of ritual and the participants' understanding of it must be addressed. Only then can the history of the two most celebrated processions, those of Holy Week and Corpus Christi, be surveyed.

Celebrations like those which Ruth Anderson witnessed in Zamora had first appeared in the late Middle Ages in response to shifts in the religious and social climate. As the rites evolved, they continued to reflect these currents and attitudes, some of which differ markedly from those elsewhere in Europe and the United States. These customs originate in a Spanish perception where faith and the structure of daily life are linked and experienced as a whole. For Spanish communities, the events serve as both personal and public expressions of faith, and they elicit a powerful response both from participants and audience, which by its intensity reveals its relevance to the individuals. Furthermore, the processions frequently involve secular authorities; in many, key figures from the municipal government – councilmen, magistrates, and constabulary – all march wearing the insignias of their offices. As the men walk by in groups ranked by their official capacity, the rites also become civic events, which include definitions of social values and, even at times, of a political system. The spectacle they present thus offers both participants and audience a way to understand the world and their role in it.

On a structural level such processions resemble other religious rituals in that they consist of repeated formulaic actions which inspire strong emotional responses.[1] In fact, almost every visitor to Spain has commented with amazement on the intensity with which the participants and community experience these events. Like most rituals, these processions are related to or directed at unseen powers, which are frequently, but not exclusively, sacred; in this case, they comprise a significant part of the community's relation to God as experienced within the Catholic Church. They also proclaim a solidarity and community in face of what may seem threatening and mysterious.

These processions should also be seen as devotions within the liturgical calendar set by the Catholic Church. The calendar calls for two sets of observances. The first occurs at moments of transition in an individual's life and marks a change in his status within the community, seen most notably in the ceremonies of baptism, confirmation, marriage, and funeral services. The other, more communal in nature, consists of liturgical seasons and holidays that are repeated annually and honor aspects of Christian faith: Christ's life and death, the Virgin's life, devotions to patron saints, or theological concepts. The most important parts of this cycle focus on retelling Christ's life. This begins with the Christmas season which runs from Christmas (December 25), the feast commemorating Christ's birth, to Epiphany (January 6), the day marking the arrival and homage of the three kings. Next follows the season of Lent, in which the faithful prepare themselves by prayer, fasting, and almsgiving to celebrate the mysteries commemorated in the holidays of Holy Week and Easter (depending on the calendar, it can fall anytime from March 22 to April 25). Holy Week begins with Palm Sunday, the day commemorating Christ's triumphal entry into Jerusalem on the eve of Passover. It continues with Maundy Thursday which marks the Last Supper and the institution of the Eucharist, the sacrament by which He makes salvation available to all. The following day, Good Friday, commemorates His sufferings and death on the cross. Finally, Easter Sunday celebrates Christ's resurrection and the promise to save all mankind. Forty and fifty days after Easter Sunday, the season concludes with the feasts of Ascension and Pentecost which retell Christ's ascent into heaven and his gift of the Holy Spirit to the apostles. Eleven days later comes Corpus Christi, a feast dedicated to the Eucharist as a manifestation of Christ's body. This day soon overshadowed Pentecost in the brilliance of its celebration. The remaining major holidays consist of the Assumption (August 15) which honors the Virgin's miraculous rise into heaven on her death, and then the feasts of All Saints' and All Souls' day (November 1 and 2 respectively), the first of which honors the community of Saints and the second the Christian dead. Within this cycle of holidays, the religious processions of statues through the streets on Holy Week, Corpus Christi, and the Assumption mark moments of exceptional religious significance, celebrating, as they do, solemn moments in the life of Christ and the Virgin or important theological concepts.

This calendar shaped the experience of time. It consolidated the commemoration of Christ's life and death within the first six months of the year, the growing season, and left the remaining six months reasonably empty. By aligning Christmas and Easter to the progression of the seasons, it also established a link to the natural world which underscored the message. Spaniards doubtless appreciated the impact of this association even more keenly in past centuries when their economy depended heavily on agriculture and the seasons.

The processions of Holy Week and Corpus Christi were not the only religious rituals celebrated during the late Middle Ages and the Early Modern Era. Elaborate processions could occur and, on occasion, plays might be performed on other high holy days, such as Christmas or All Souls' day. For instance on All Souls' day, a high mass was held in the Seville cathedral, after which the celebrant and canons would process through the church to say prayers over numerous tombs of their distinguished predecessors, the prelates and prebends of the cathedral.[2] Highly revered statues of the Virgin or Christ might also be involved in ceremonies when a natural disaster, such as a drought or a plague, threatened the community and divine intercession was sought.[3]

Of all these celebrations, however, those held during Holy Week and Corpus Christi soon became the most significant.[4] Spaniards had begun to observe the feasts with processions as early as the late fifteenth century, but they became increasingly elaborate in the sixteenth century. In their message, the holidays differ notably: the first commemorates Christ's Passion and Resurrection while the second glorifies the Eucharist. The rituals performed on these days reflect the distinct religious concepts celebrated, while the organization of the events evokes various levels of participation. Confraternities, religious brotherhoods dedicated to perform charitable acts, were at the heart of Holy Week. Each group arranged its own processions in which its members would perform public acts of contrition as they accompanied the confraternity's statues and floats depicting scenes of Christ's Passion or the Virgin's anguish. On Corpus Christi, on the other hand, the church hierarchy organized a single procession for the Host in which ecclesiastical and municipal authorities would march. Included in the festivities were figures, floats, and plays sponsored by local guilds and confraternities, but these too would focus on the theme of the holiday, the triumph of the Host.

Although thematically and structurally different, the celebration of both holidays employed ritual and theatrical elements. To this extent, the evolution of their celebration is interrelated. At the same time, the history of these rituals is intertwined with political and religious developments.

Of the two, Corpus Christi was initially celebrated with the most splendor. The theological concept, the veneration of the consecrated host, enjoyed widespread popularity in the later Middle Ages. Established by the Papacy in 1264, the feast had flourished as devotion of the Eucharist grew in this period.[5] Townspeople, gathered together in guilds or confraternities, pooled their resources to build floats for tableaux or plays for the festival. Competition quickly ensued between these groups as each one tried to outdo the other by providing the most spectacular contribution.

Changes in Christianity during the sixteenth century, however, affected the holiday's celebration. Where Europe had previously been united as one Church, critics of its beliefs and practices now broke off and formed the Protestant Churches. As they spread their new faith, their success inspired the Catholic Reformation, a movement in which the Catholic Church reevaluated its dogma and rituals.[6] One of the most contentious articles of faith had been the nature of the Eucharist. As Catholic reformers responded to Protestant attacks, the celebration of Corpus Christi, the holiday devoted to this embattled dogma, elicited renewed interest. Ecclesiastical authorities, particularly in Spain, carefully supervised the holiday, arranging for elaborate plays and processions that proclaimed the message of a militant and triumphant Church.[7] They had realized the didactic value in holding such events; now, they wished to control the message that emerged, above all to eliminate any heresy that might result from unmonitored theatrical productions.

fig. 1
Juan de Mesa, *Jesús del Gran Poder*, 1620, Capilla del Gran Poder, Seville (Photo courtesy of Arxiu Mas)

Even as the Church was clamping down on the celebration of Corpus Christi, popular devotion was finding a new outlet in the celebrations of Holy Week. Obviously, the Death and Resurrection of Christ represent the central mystery of the Christian faith and, as such, would always receive significant attention. Initially, the celebration of Corpus Christi served as a model with its succession of floats and dramas subsidized by guilds and confraternities all of whom competed with each other. Several factors, however, made Holy Week even more gripping to Spaniards at this time, and two distinctive elements soon appeared in the processions: the *pasos*, the multifigural floats of religious statues designed specially for this occasion (fig. 1), and the hooded penitents who accompany these figures.

The *pasos* grew out of a response to shifts in Spanish religious theater. Early drama includes texts for Easter plays, and evidence also survives of rituals reenacting the Descent from the Cross. Ecclesiastical reform in the sixteenth century, however, ended most such practices. The same clerics who worried about the orthodoxy of plays performed at Corpus Christi turned their attention towards those staged at Easter.[8] These efforts led to the elimination of such plays and their replacement with the figural *pasos* which the viewer sees today. In addition to ecclesiastical pressure, the shift reflects practical considerations. Whereas the plays could only be performed a limited number of times and in spaces that would accommodate a large audience, the statues on the floats told their story without interruption for the procession's entire route. Moreover, they seemed a more decorous representation of this most holy mystery. Because actors were reputedly immoral, an unintentional irony could undermine the dignity of the events enacted. For instance, during the performance of a play of the Annunciation after the archangel Gabriel had announced to the Virgin Mary that she would conceive the savior, her reply "How will this be done since I do not know man?" convulsed the audience with laughter since they knew of her liaison with another actor.[9] A procession of *pasos* avoided such a response. By the seventeenth century, religious processions accompanied by floats were established in Seville and Valladolid.

The second feature, the flagellant penitents, made their first appearance in the late Middle Ages. Such processions had occurred throughout the fifteenth century in Spain, but confraternities expressly dedicated to such penance are only documented towards the end of the century. Among the earliest were those in Zamora where confraternities held processions on Maundy Thursday.[10] As the practice spread rapidly throughout Spain, the number of participants grew, and by the late sixteenth century, large confraternities of flagellants both in Seville and Valladolid were taking elaborate *pasos* out as acts of penitence.

The popularity of such public acts of contrition corresponds to contemporary developments in faith. The Early Modern Era witnessed a growing emphasis on the sacrifice of Christ and as part of the trend, sympathy for the Virgin's suffering at the sight of her son's ordeal also grew.[11] In this climate, self-flagellation became an appealing way to empathize with Christ, recreating as much as possible his experience and offering a public act of atonement for one's sins. Many thus found it the most convincing way to appeal to God. Further, because a majority of Spaniards already lived a hard life, they hoped these extreme acts would convince God of their repentance and secure pardon for the community.

These processions were grounded in several popular institutions and beliefs, some of which gave both the Crown and Church pause. A series of edicts concerning costume clearly reveal their concerns that processions were not purely religious. The penitents' robes and conical hats proved one of the earliest sticking points. For instance, the phrasing of sixteenth-century statutes from Castile suggests that it was a desire to conceal the identity of those atoning for their sins which lay behind the requirement that they wear hooded outfits.[12] Nonetheless, aristocratic confraternities introduced more elaborate costumes with ruff collars, velvet robes, and conical hoods, thereby disclosing their rank if not their individual identity. Similar developments must have occurred in Seville because a church synod of 1604 required that the dress of the penitents be simple and uniform with no signs of ostentation or identity.[13] Whereas early sixteenth-century images depict a variety of costumes for Spanish penitents, the most distinctive feature, the *capirote*, the conical hood worn today, was already in use by the 1580s. In the late Middle Ages, *capirote* referred to a hood worn by mourners at funerals, and its use had apparently been transferred to penitential processions by 1586.[14] Moreover, the costume had acquired such fame that a Flemish engraver, A. de Bruyn, included a print of it in an album of costumes of the world, 1581-86 (fig. 2).[15] His image clearly shows the pointed cap, although without the pasteboard below that kept the *capirote* pointing upwards.

Given Spanish society's rigidity and emphasis on rank, the blurring of such distinctions in the dress of the penitents made a strong statement of equal humility, creating in effect a brotherhood in atonement. But the Church had further reasons to insist on the participant's anonymity. By practicing such severe flagellation and other acts of mortification, those marching in procession became heroes for the community. Ecclesiastical authorities were anxious to curb the practice which sought and basked in this admiration because it detracted from the value of the act and reduced it to vainglorious achievement. Moreover, as such displays grew increasingly popular and some men believed it appealed to women, the Church felt further need to impose control. Still, the Seville synod shows that even when penitents wore hoods, authorities worried that individuals might still carry some sign of identity.

The austerity imposed on costume did not, however, carry over to other aspects of the processions. In the province of Zamora, these events grew increasingly more extreme as membership in penitential confraternities rose and with it the number of flagellants who marched at these times. Prestige was not only accorded to the individual penitent but also to those confraternities with large numbers of penitents. In Seville, this pressure led smaller brotherhoods to pay people to march as flagellants, another practice the synod of 1604 sought to abolish.[16] Throughout Spain, confraternities also made a concerted effort to enhance the splendor of these moments in the number and quality of their floats. In particular, documents and traveller's accounts testify to the growing opulence of those in Seville, Valladolid, and Zamora.

Other restrictions which the Church attempted to impose suggest further concerns with early processions. The 1604 synod in Seville wished to regulate the organization and scheduling of these events so as to eliminate those held at night and their accompanying disturbances. Without proper planning, two confraternities might find themselves trying to enter a street or square at the same moment, and such a scene could easily lead to riots unbecoming of the holy days. There was good reason to worry, since this had occurred, and in one instance brothers had used not only staffs but concealed weapons to break through the other procession.[17] Further, authorities feared that hooded figures roaming at night would take advantage of the anonymity of their costume to commit crimes. The bishop was also anxious to eliminate any competition between these processions and the formal rites celebrated in the church. Nonetheless, these issues remained problematic. After a particularly riotous celebration in 1622, the government attempted a massive reorganization of the confraternities. It reiterated the 1604 synod's rulings regarding the order of processions and costume while also establishing a series of fines and punishments for those who failed to obey. Similar problems had also arisen in

fig. 2
A. de Bruyn, *Spanish Flagellants*, Engraving from *Omnia Pene Europae, Asiae, Aphricae Atque Americae Gentium Habitus*. ca. 1600 reprint by M. Colin of edition issued by Bosscher 1581-86. (Photo courtesy of The Hispanic Society of America)

Valladolid. There the order of processions spawned numerous lawsuits as confraternities vied for the best times, until the archbishop settled the question.[18]

The role of women in processions shifted in this period. Women had initially been allowed to walk with the men to console and light the way, just as Mary and Veronica had accompanied Christ as He carried the Cross. Such participation troubled reformers who enacted a series of measures that gradually eliminated it. In a royal decree, Philip II (1527-98) worried that hooded costumes might provide an opportunity for immoral conduct so he ordered female penitents to uncover their faces.[19] The Seville synod went further and banned them from the procession, thereby relegating them to the role of passive observers.[20]

The efforts by the Crown and Church to regulate processions point out their popularity and the confraternities' importance. In fact, brotherhoods played a significant role in the social structure of cities such as Seville, Valladolid, and Zamora. Confraternities had existed during the late Middle Ages as a way for laypeople to practice their religion. Funded by membership fees and endowments, these groups provided charity for the poor and said prayers and masses for their deceased brothers. They also played a part in keeping the peace by maintaining order among members and holding banquets to promote good spirits. After the Catholic Reformation, the Church tried to regulate confraternities more closely so they became less social clubs and more religious. Ecclesiastics hoped to subdue the exuberance of the traditional banquet, the parades, the floats, and the bull fights so they became subsidiary to rosary devotions and prayer vigils. Nonetheless, participation in Holy Week processions became the primary focus of many confraternities.

The elaboration of Holy Week celebrations corresponds to a broader social development in which ceremony and ritual took on a greater role in Spanish culture during the seventeenth century. Similarly, the observance of Corpus Christi, the other major holiday to include a procession, did not lag far behind. Its evolution reflects political and religious values which combined to shape the day's message uniquely. Since the kings of Castile and their government identified themselves so closely with divine authority and the Catholic Church, the holiday marked not only the triumph of the Eucharist and the Church but also that of the monarchs who supported it. In effect, the day offered a powerful statement of Christian solidarity in both religious and political spheres. The celebrations were also distinguished by the inclusion of carnivalesque elements – popular dances, a figure of the *tarrasca* (a mythical beast part-serpent part-dragon), and giants. Although they may seem more striking, the political imagery of the festival was no less important to a contemporary audience.

Cities throughout Spain celebrated Corpus Christi on a lavish scale (fig. 3). Because those in Granada have been thoroughly studied, they offer a detailed picture.[21] The municipal government went to great lengths to ensure that the city be beautiful for that day, issuing prohibitions that nothing be thrown onto the streets where the procession would pass. Decorations were hung from windows and eventually a path was prepared. The municipality erected ephemeral altars (five by 1661) along the route where the procession would stop to place the host and say special prayers. The decoration of these altars could include images of events related to the history of the sacrament. In addition, numerous arches (twenty in 1632) were raised while private citizens might set up individual altars along the route with elaborate paintings and sculpture. Some of these included complicated constructions such as hydraulic devices, games, and improvised gardens. The most intricate of the ephemeral monuments – a gallery – was built in one of the city's principal squares, the Plaza Bibarrambla. Lavishly decorated with elaborate schemes, this structure offers some of the most vivid evidence of the link between religion and politics in the celebration of the day.[22] By the eighteenth century, some programs had turned to local history: they expressly recast the Castilian reconquest of Granada from the Moors in 1492 as a religious feat, thereby making the triumph one for Spanish Catholic arms which had marched under the banner of the Eucharist.

The evening before Corpus Christi, the city would be illuminated and a festive air pervaded. Vespers for celebrations the following day were heralded with the ringing of bells and the firing of artillery. Figures from the next day's procession, the *tarrasca* and the giants, sometimes riding on horseback, roamed the streets. Notwithstanding their roots in carnival, these characters were interpreted as symbols of evil and the seven deadly sins which would later be routed by the sacrament.

fig. 3
Corpus Christi Procession leaving the Cathedral, Seville ca. 1930. More recent celebrations, like this one, offer a glimpse of earlier rites. (Photo courtesy of The Hispanic Society of America)

The celebrations of the holiday involved both the religious and civic authorities, thereby emphasizing the broad nature of the event. Figures from both the municipal government and the ecclesiastic hierarchy attended a high mass in the cathedral. Afterwards the procession set out in a carefully arranged order which continued the message of political and religious harmony: first the giants and *tarrasca*; then local confraternities; priests from the diocese and town; carts and dances; cathedral chapter; the host in its *custodia* (monstrance); the archbishop; the municipal government; and at the end, the military regiment of the province. Along the way, the procession would stop and pray at the temporary altars. The importance attached to the etiquette of these ceremonies emerges in a longstanding feud between the archbishop and the town council. The problem hinged on the question of whether the archbishop could bring a chair with him on which to sit while the host was placed on these temporary altars. In particular, the town council alleged a lack of respect because the prelate turned his back on them at these moments. After the procession, actors would perform *autos*, religious plays whose didactic message corresponded to the day, namely the power of the sacrament.

Not only in Granada but throughout Spain, the processions of Corpus Christi had a long history of guild sponsorship for the construction and maintenance of the floats, tableaux, or plays. For the feast's celebrations of 1453, these organizations in Seville subsidized plays of Adam and Eve, the Epiphany, the Descent from the Cross, the Invention of the Cross, and the Conversion of Constantine. As the Spanish theater emerged, guilds turned to major playwrights. In 1543, they commissioned one of the first such authors, Lope de Rueda, to produce "an allegorical castle" on the subject of the bosom of Abraham which included Abraham, Lazarus, and six souls.[23] For a different guild in Seville, the same author composed an *auto* on the Assumption. In the seventeenth century, Pedro Calderón de la Barca, perhaps Spain's greatest dramatist of the era, raised the genre to a high literary level, making it a vehicle for a sophisticated expression of theology. In additions to plays and floats, guilds and brotherhoods subsidized and sponsored an expensive array of jugglers, dancers, and musicians.

The uneasy interaction of the official church and popular elements appears in the processions. There the archbishop and clergy would take the preeminent position, but one suspects the public preferred the entertainment provided by the guilds. In a holiday where such features threatened to overwhelm the event, the Church's consistent desire to control the celebrations should not be surprising. The Church regulated *autos* and guild participation to prevent diffusion of bad doctrine or prevent it from turning into secular carnival. Not all edicts were well-received. The dances proved to be one of the most popular features. Their defenders justified them by comparing them to biblical passages where dancing had marked joyous celebrations. Nonetheless, a reforming archbishop of Seville attempted to eliminate dances performed in the cathedral.[24] His actions met with extreme hostility and resistance, to the point where a crude bomb was discovered in the cathedral confessional where he was scheduled to hear confessions.

Although the rituals celebrated at Holy Week and Corpus Christi attained a high degree of splendor during the seventeenth and early eighteenth centuries, the celebrations evolved over time as the political and religious climate changed. Most notably, subsequent generations took up the reforms which their predecessors had been unable to enact. Under Charles III (1716-88), government policies reflected the rationalist philosophy of the Enlightenment, and secular authorities now undertook a campaign more extensive than any previously attempted to control the excesses of such holidays.[25] The king, his ministers, and Spanish bishops worried that an uneducated and credulous mass were celebrating these days with customs that reflected superstition more than faith. Like previous regimes, they also distrusted processions for the disorder and crimes that could easily ensue as penitents wandered the streets at night. Thus in 1777 Charles III moved to reform religious practices by banning penitential flagellation, nocturnal processions, and dancing in the churches before the images. Regarding penitential flagellation, the king says that "it serves not to edify or inspire contrition, but provokes scorn in the wise, diversion and high-spirits in the youths, amazement, confusion, and fear in children and women. To these ends, and others even more damaging, it is directed by those who do it and [they perform these acts] not to set a good example and atone for their sins." He exhorts those "who might possess a true spirit of contrition and repentance to choose other more rational and secret ways that are less apparent with the advice and direction of their confessors." Strikingly, this final appeal shows how the king, like most of his enlightened reformers, considered himself a good Catholic engaged in purifying the practice of the faith.

When the edict was pronounced in Seville, the archbishop added an order forbidding the penitents to conceal their faces under their hoods.[26] Similarly, municipal authorities in both Valladolid and Seville followed the monarch's lead and issued their own decrees restricting Holy Week processions to hours of daylight.[27] Not surprisingly, these measures met with sullen resistance and confraternities either flouted them or looked for loopholes, but the new legislation ultimately undermined the processions. In fact, this moment marks a shift during which many such observances were curtailed if not discontinued completely. Moreover, numerous confraternities throughout Spain saw their numbers decrease and their processions grow less splendid.

Charles III's decree and the reaction it elicited reveal a growing shift between liberal and conservative attitudes towards religious practices. The former believed that the popular elements obscured the true religious spirit of the holidays, whereas the latter were reluctant to relinquish these traditions. Their resistance to the government's measures suggests the popularity of these rites in spite of the authorities' reservations. In particular, the explicitness of the king's instructions banning dances in churches suggests the length some would go to undermine the decree: "Do not allow dances in the churches, their porches, or cemeteries, nor in front of the saints' images after they have been removed for this purpose to another place under the pretext of celebrating their festivities, worshipping them, or making offerings." But the reformers had also gained strength, albeit modestly. Where in the previous century the archbishop of Seville had almost been assassinated for attempting to end such practices, many more prelates had now adopted a liberal position and the king's decision met with greater support.

Enlightened moderate church reform, which had been viable only under Charles III, ceased to be an option as subsequent political events polarized the question. The first half of the nineteenth century witnessed a series of tumultuous events in Spain with the French invasion under Napoleon, the subsequent Spanish uprising, and the Peninsular War of 1808-12. After the French were ejected and the Bourbon monarchy restored, the political order remained shaky as liberals and conservatives fought to define the nation. In this climate, resentment of the power and privileges of the Church grew stronger, and politicians hotly debated its role in Spanish life. Liberals, who had always distrusted the Church's influence, now hoped to weaken it substantially and solve economic problems by selling off its assets in the disamortization acts of 1834 and 1841. All of these events took their toll on religious celebrations.

The reforms effected by liberal governments had severed official ties to the Church, and the state now took control of public institutions previously administered by the Church. Nonetheless, it had not changed the traditional culture as most citizens experienced it. Thus when more conservative regimes took power, the way was open for a rapprochement with the Church. This in fact occurred with the creation of a constitutional monarchy in 1875 after years of political instability, and a Catholic revival followed in the late nineteenth and early twentieth centuries.[28] Social, economic, and regional factors, however, limited the extent of this revival. Most broadly, ties to Europe had permitted constant access to contemporary thought which fostered anticlericalism and later led to a secularism that pervaded many aspects of life. More than anything else, this prevented the Church from regaining the prominence it had previously enjoyed. Still, it devoted itself to a campaign of evangelization and education which had its greatest success among the middle and upper classes. Elsewhere, the results were more uneven: Old Castile continued a conservative Catholic adherence while parts of Andalusia, although Catholic in name, seemed less devout in practice.[29] Further, agrarian poor and industrial labor proved to be a hotbed for discontent, often with anarchist or republican tendencies. This resulted from distrust of an institution that seemed to have abandoned them and identified with those sectors of society which made their lives difficult.

With the Catholic revival, many religious processions and the organizations which had sponsored them experienced a new vitality. Among other measures, the Church fostered more groups for laypeople, such as confraternities which now enjoyed a resurgence in importance with the revitalization of existing ones and the foundation of new ones. Clerics also emphasized the formulaic and ritual elements of the faith by promoting greater awareness of the sacraments as well as religious processions and pilgrimages. At approximately the same time, civic authorities also began to play a more supportive role as they saw an incentive in the celebration of religious holidays: to foster an awareness of local customs and help the region's economy.

The history of Granada's celebration of Corpus Christi in the nineteenth century fully reflects these changing currents.[30] By the beginning of the century, celebrations had decayed to such a point that they required repeated reorganizations in 1817, 1820, 1852, and 1859. The municipal government was by now looking to revive the festival so as to revitalize the city's image and its economy. In 1883, it organized a splendid celebration which would subsequently become famous. As planned, the day was no longer a local holiday but one directed at the entire region. The city arranged for widespread publicity and special promotional train fares to Granada from other parts of Andalusia. Nor was the day simply one of processions and festivities in honor of the Eucharist as the city

fig. 4
Holy Week Procession in Valladolid 1923 with Gregorio Fernández's *Paso* of the *Flagellation of Christ* (Photo courtesy of The Hispanic Society of America)

broadened its appeal by organizing exhibitions of embroidery by upper class women and concerts in the Palace of Charles V.

A comparable resurgence occurred in the Holy Week celebrations in Seville in the nineteenth century. With the Church-sponsored revival, confraternities grew again in numbers, while the municipal government, with the backing of the middle class, began to subsidize the celebrations so as to foster an event that would bring tourists to the city.[31] Perhaps the most striking signs of renewal occurred in Valladolid. In 1923, Holy Week processions were organized that included seventeenth-century *pasos* which had not gone out in years (fig. 4).[32] The way this came about reveals much about the significance attached to the religious event. The committee responsible included not only the archbishop and civic authorities, but also the director of the Valladolid museum and other art historians. One of these admitted that the "processions will never become what they once were."[33] Further, he acknowledged that whereas the floats had constituted a popular expression of religion in their time, the procession of these works now served equally as an expression of art. To make it possible to appreciate the *pasos* all year round, the government arranged for them to be displayed in galleries specially set aside in the National Museum in Valladolid. The government of the time was a conservative and Catholic regime, anxious to support such a tribute to Spain's traditional faith and artistry.

The interpretation of these festivals and, even more importantly, the role of the Church, however, remained contested in political circles. Whereas the revival of such celebrations owed much to the renewed Catholicism, it also corresponded to the efforts of various regimes to link themselves with the Church. The constitutional monarchy and the subsequent dictatorship of Primo de Rivera (1923-30) officially maintained the institutions of the Church, while many liberal politicians also considered themselves Catholics. This precarious balance, however, could not last much longer. The extent of the Church's renewal and influence, particularly in the field of education, inspired resentment, and an anticlerical movement grew stronger both in liberal and republican parties. The virulence of this protest appears in Barcelona's *semana trágica* of 1909.

Demonstrating against the war in Morocco and its draft, a mob destroyed at least eighty buildings belonging to various church institutions, while generally leaving other potential targets – government officials, military, police and wealthy individuals – alone. Simultaneously, conservatives were defining an equally hard-line to the right. As this wing came to see the needs of Spain in terms of ideological traditionalism, it longed to reestablish the preeminence of the old faith.

The rift between the two sides took on greater animosity when the Spanish Republic was established (1931) and passed severe laws limiting church power. In this climate, religious ceremonies such as Holy Week processions were inevitably drawn into the fray, but sometimes in unexpected ways. When the republican mayor of Seville attempted to arrange for a splendid Holy Week procession in 1932, conservative elements, including the archdiocese, opposed him with a boycott designed to embarrass his government; in the end, only one confraternity attempted to take its procession out where it was received with an emotive and supportive display.[34] The following year no processions occurred; in 1934, a number returned; and after that they were back to full strength.[35] Perhaps even more interesting than the efforts by conservative Catholics to block the processions was their subsequent rewriting of the events in which they reversed themselves. According to this, it was an outrage that the processions had not occurred, and obviously no mention was made of their opposition. Rather, the confraternities had not ventured forth because they feared for their safety under the lawless rule of the republicans. In the end, blame fell on the very party which had done everything it could to facilitate the processions.

These developments, however, lay in the future when Ruth Anderson traveled to Spain. Still, they did not lie far below the surface when she photographed various celebrations in Zamora, Villalcampo, Jerez de los Caballeros, and La Alberca. The festivals she witnessed could have been understood as expressions of religion, colored with political overtones and linked to a sense of regional identity. At the same time, others appreciated them for their folklore or potential to boost local commerce.

Today, many of these celebrations continue to form an integral part of Spanish social life. Nowhere is this truer than in the Holy Week processions of Andalusia. These rituals form part of an impassioned view of the world, and communities experience these events directly rather than observe them.[36] As the country evolved, this region has developed an individual identity that manifests itself particularly in these rites. Viewing the world through an emotional and fatalistic lens, many Andalusians have attributed their poverty to destiny and a powerful elite which has left them poor. Thus they readily identify with the unjustly accused Christ and his mother, the Virgin Mary, whose sufferings become the focus of Holy Week. This emphasis results in a peculiar trait: the celebrations end with little, if any, reference to the Resurrection. Furthermore, the rituals of Holy Week are embedded in a system that affects life the whole year round since the confraternities which organize processions also provide a social structure by defining groups within the community.

Chapter 2

Art and Processions in Spain and the New World

Although many writers have left striking accounts of religious processions, perhaps more dramatic testimony appears in visual sources. A painting such as that by Philip Villamil, *"Los Nazarenos": The Penitents' Procession*, Seville, ca. 1860 (Cat. 56: The Hispanic Society of America, LA1074, fig. 5), vividly evokes these events in its rendering of penitents, crowds, and the statue with its canopy.[1] As the spectators watch the hooded figures holding candles and the image of the Virgin advancing, Villamil captures both the drama of a religious procession and the festive atmosphere of well-dressed people gathered for a parade. Still, his composition could never be accounted objective reportage with its emphasis on the elegant ladies and its slightly exaggerated depiction of *nazarenos*. More broadly, as the work of an Englishman (active 1838-70) who specialized in Andalusian scenes, the canvas falls within the genre of travel art in which the painter, an outsider, portrays the custom of an exotic and foreign land. Nonetheless, the painting suggests the prominence which processional sculpture attained during Holy Week. Similarly, Ruth Anderson's photographs reveal the important role statues played on these holidays and the intense adoration they received.

fig. 5
Philip Villamil,
"Los Nazarenos": The Penitents' Procession, Seville,
ca. 1860
(Photo courtesy of The Hispanic Society of America)

Given their importance in these rites, the statues and floats require further study. Because the works can easily appear strange both for their style and role as devotional objects, an examination of their artistic tradition and function offers a context in which to interpret them. At the same time, a more detailed understanding of such pieces also enhances the appreciation of the religious observances in which they participated.

Processional imagery, both the multifigural floats and single figures taken out during Holy Week and other feasts, developed in the context of Spanish sculpture from the sixteenth to the eighteenth centuries. The examination of such works presents difficulties, primarily because the field has received little attention outside of Spain.[2] Furthermore, processional art has until recently been overlooked as many scholars relegated these works to a secondary status.[3] In its day, however, the genre enjoyed an importance which the present neglect belies. In fact, such images played a central role in religious art, and the sculptors exerted their talents to the fullest in works that combined naturalism and emotionalism.

Artists exploited these qualities to create the impression that the religious event or figure depicted is physically present, thereby enhancing the work's impact and the response it elicits from the viewer. To strengthen this effect, sculptors designed figures that could be clothed and accommodate accessories such as glass eyes, jewelry, weapons, a crown of thorns, or rope as required. If the figure were not dressed in real textiles, the artist might model sized cloth (fabric saturated with plaster or a similar substance to stiffen it) over the wood armature and thus create the illusion of drapery. In their search for expressive intensity and immediacy, sculptors used such attachments and features not only in processional imagery but in all manner of figures. Thus Spanish sculpture in general is characterized by an additive quality which has probably further prejudiced its study since purists consider the works a mixed genre.

The creation of such processional images and more broadly of all sculpture reflects the religious climate of the period. Beginning in the sixteenth century, Spain witnessed a revival of piety throughout all sectors of society. This renewal reflected the Church's efforts at reform, to answer the challenges of the Protestant Reformation, but it also corresponded to domestic needs. Under the Church's watchful eye, confraternities and other popular expressions of faith flourished. During this period, many made extensive gifts to religious institutions while those who could founded new monasteries, convents, and religious colleges. These developments had an impact on art because, whether renovating an existing space or constructing a new one, the demand for religious images grew. The function they played was reexamined as well: following the edicts of the Council of Trent (1545-63), the Church advocated a greater role for them as a tool to instruct and inspire laypeople. Consequently, more works began to appear not only in churches and monasteries but also in private homes. At the same time, ecclesiastical authorities established guidelines for images and a process to regulate them for doctrinal correctness.

Other factors affected the way people interpreted such images. On the most intimate level, many writers now recommended programs of meditation which focused the believer's attention on the holy mysteries and could ultimately lead to a deeper relation with God. The most famous of these were the Spiritual Exercises of St. Ignatius, but many authors offered alternative manuals. In particular, the lives of mystics like St. Teresa or St. John of the Cross presented examples where contemplation had brought the believer into a union with God. Although exceptional figures in this regard, St. Teresa and St. John of the Cross attracted many followers and founded several religious houses, which further demonstrates the growing popularity and relevance of these programs. The intimate and emotional nature of this meditation doubtless made people more susceptible to the expressive qualities in religious art. In fact, St. Teresa herself describes her response to a statue of an *Ecce homo*: it "represented the much wounded Christ and was very devotional so that beholding it I was utterly distressed seeing him that way, for it well represented what he suffered for us."[4] The image filled her with such remorse that she threw herself down before it with an "outpouring of tears."

Only by understanding the greater prominence of religious art and the fervent faith which sustained it can Spanish sculpture be understood. The market called for a growing number of works, but it also required artists to repeat compositions sanctioned by tradition and approved by ecclesiastical authorities. Significantly, patrons prized devotional images for those qualities that evoked an emotional response and embodied a preconceived image.[5] Each sculptor could alter it somewhat, but in the end, the figure had to conform to the type. The artist thus had to elicit an emotional impact while adhering to a prescribed composition. The division between type and sculptor's hand cannot, however, always be defined so easily; the artists' formal predispositions may have lead them to imagine different poses and expressions which in turn affected the realization of the type.

Within these parameters, Spain saw a flowering of talented sculptors from the sixteenth through eighteenth centuries. Throughout this period, artists employed a progression of styles: the Italianate and classical Renaissance of the sixteenth century, the naturalistic and intensely expressive Baroque of the seventeenth century, and finally the delicate and refined Rococo of the eighteenth century. Within this sequence, three centers stand out: Valladolid, Seville, and Granada. In the first city, Alonso Berruguete (1489-1561) and Juan de Juni (ca. 1507-77) created major works in the sixteenth century while Gregorio Fernández (1576-1636) established many important models for the following century. Perhaps sculpture flourished nowhere more than in Seville during the seventeenth century as the city sustained a high level of activity dominated by Juan Bautista Martínez Montañés (1568-1649) and Juan de Mesa (1583-1627) in the early years and Pedro de Roldán (1624-99) and his daughter Luisa (1652-1706) towards the end. In Granada, Diego de Siloe (d. 1563) introduced many elements of the Italian Renaissance in the sixteenth century, and subsequent sculptors, most notably Pedro de Mena (1628-88) and the workshop of the Mora family (Bernardo de Mora: 1614-84 and his sons José de Mora: 1642-1724 and Diego de Mora: 1658-1729), made the city a major center of sculpture in the seventeenth century.

The creation of processional art thus occurred as part of a thriving art form, and sculptors created *pasos* throughout the peninsula. In particular, documents from Seville and Valladolid reveal that the finest artists had no qualms in working on these: for instance, Gregorio Fernández created two in Valladolid, the *Pietá* and the *Descent from the Cross* which must be ranked among the masterpieces of Spanish seventeenth-century sculpture. Other works by this artist, such as his *Christ Tied to the Column*, bridge the gap of processional and devotional sculpture since they serve both functions. They can be taken out in processions while remaining on an altar for the rest of the year. (As *pasos* had grown more elaborate, many multifigural ensembles were simply stored by their owners until Holy Week, while in others, only the central statues of Christ or the Virgin might be placed on an altar.) Processional works, however, trace the same pattern as the rites themselves; from the sixteenth to the early eighteenth centuries, artists produced rich and complex works, but this was followed by a slight decline in stylistic inventiveness and scale of production. Nonetheless, the tradition remained alive as sculptors and painters continued to produce new images while renovating and updating existing ones. In the 1940s, for instance, the celebrated Spanish sculptor, Mariano

Benlliure (1862-1947), carved a number of religious pieces designed for processions, including some for the city of Zamora.⁶

Unfortunately, it has not been possible to include processional sculpture in this exhibition. Few examples survive outside Spain, and a recent census, admittedly incomplete, of Spanish sculpture lists no *pasos* in North American public collections.⁷ In part, this situation reflects the functional nature of the pieces. Many works remain in the churches where they continue to serve their original function. Moreover, once a confraternity or church replaces them, the works are discarded and do not pass readily into use elsewhere. Nonetheless, several works have been selected to reflect the style, imagery, and technique of the images taken out on those days.

fig. 6
Anonymous Castilian, *The Deposition*, ca. 1525
(Photo courtesy of The Hispanic Society of America)

The earliest object, the anonymous relief *The Deposition*, ca. 1500–25 (Cat. 63: The Hispanic Society of America, D14, fig. 6) evokes the intense emotional impact which images of Christ's Passion could achieve.⁸ This sculpture suggests not only the intensity of religious expression of the early sixteenth century but also the inherent dramatism which inspired the Holy Week processions, shortly about to take shape. The depiction of the dead Christ mourned by the Virgin and Saints appears frequently in contemporary altars, but it is suggestive to recall that at the same time religious ceremonies reenacting the burial of Christ were also being developed. Finally, such a relief may have played a further role: as sculptors were called on to develop multifigural compositions for processions, a work like this would have served as a model.

fig. 7
Anonymous Andalusian, *Simon of Cyrene* [?], ca. 1670-1700
(Photo courtesy of The Hispanic Society of America)

Two further pieces suggest some of the demands which the creation of *pasos* made on artists. Carved by an anonymous Andalusian master, *Simon of Cyrene* [?], ca. 1670-1700 (Cat. 64: The Hispanic Society of America, D31, fig. 7) represents a figure with articulated arms that

fig. 8
Anonymous Andalusian, *Saint Joseph* [?], ca. 1725-50 (Photo courtesy of The Hispanic Society of America)

enable the piece to be maneuvered into a desired pose.⁹ Whereas this figure may originally have belonged to a small-scale ensemble depicting Christ Carrying the Cross, the Descent from the Cross, or Entombment, it shows how larger figures on the *pasos* could be manipulated. In fact, the preparations of the floats for each year included the arrangement of the figures and perhaps the addition of new ones. Similarly, the Andalusian statue of *Saint Joseph* [?], ca. 1725-50, (Cat. 65: The Hispanic Society of America, D6, fig. 8) demonstrates the powerful effect achieved by color and vivid polychromy.¹⁰ By the time the sculptor created this figure, the technique was well-developed, and the artist took full advantage of its possibilities to enhance the impact of his elegant figure with an opulent decoration.

Christ's Passion and the Virgin's anguish at his pain and death dominated processions in a series of *pasos* of Christ Carrying the Cross, the Crucifixion, or the *Mater Dolorosa*, Sorrowing Virgin. The iconography of these statues, however, did not remain static but was subject to subtle modifications. These changes appear most visibly in southern Spain where the focus increasingly fell on the suffering of Christ and the Virgin while images of the Resurrection became rarer. Similarly, the taste for ensembles that expressed allegorical concepts like Christ's Triumph over sin, evil, and death gave way after the seventeenth century, although a handful of such *pasos* survive (including one which Anderson photographed in Jerez de los Caballeros.) In Seville, the decoration of individual floats experienced changes that affected their import.¹¹ Images of Christ Carrying the Cross were stripped of subsidiary figures thereby focusing on the Savior; even in those which include Simon of Cyrene who assists in bearing the cross, the emphasis still falls on Christ. In contrast, Crucifixion ensembles remained multifigural, with additions reaching the point where the figure of Christ seemed to disappear among all those present. Renovations also transformed *pasos* of the Virgin, almost turning them into mini-altars rather than tableaux. Although they continued to depict her anguish, these images increasingly acquired a triumphal note. Subsidiary figures were gradually removed from floats depicting the Virgin's grief at the foot of the cross, which heightened the focus on her figure. At the same time, the statues became more regal and aloof as they acquired canopies and thrones.

These images of Christ's Passion and the Virgin's sorrows inspired numerous small-scale versions designed for private devotion. The rise of such art reflects the religious revival that had begun in the sixteenth century and illustrates the extent to which it had pervaded Spanish life. A broad range of patrons now commissioned these statues: confraternities decorated their chapels and meeting halls with such works; nuns or monks prized them as adornments for the chapels to which they retired for private contemplation; priests set them in sacristies, the rooms where they changed into their vestments, so as to seek inspiration from them before celebrating mass; and private citizens installed them in chapels or shrines in their homes. In spite of their various functions, the statues were all designed as objects for religious contemplation and therefore share a style that strives to elicit an emotional response.

Among the images of Christ's Passion, the period witnessed a rise in those depicting the Flagellation, whether Christ at the Column or immediately afterwards or yet later when Pilate presents him to the Jews, scourged and wearing a crown of thorns, in the type known as the *Ecce homo*. The popularity of such works derived from an empathy with Christ's suffering which found its most direct expression in penitential flagellation. Thus the gruesome depiction of his gaunt face contorted with pain, bleeding wounds, and sometimes welts offers a vivid realization of the pain by which he had earned salvation for mankind. On occasion, sculptors heightened the effect with details such as glass eyes, a real crown of thorns, and even real rope to bind Christ's hands.

fig. 9
Anonymous Castilian, *Ecce homo*, ca. 1600
(Photo courtesy of The Martin D'Arcy Museum of Art, Loyola University Chicago)

The first *Ecce homo* on display (Cat. 66: The Martin D'Arcy Museum of Art, Loyola University Chicago, 16.81, fig. 9) shows how a sculptor active ca. 1600 realized the theme.[12] Artistically, the work reveals a shift. The slender, graceful body recalls Italianate figures characteristic of Berruguete's followers in the second half of the sixteenth century (such as the Christ in Juan Picardo's *Deposition*, Valladolid Cathedral Museum, or that in Isidoro de Villoldo's *Flagellation*, Altar of San Bernarbé, Avila Cathedral Sacristy). Iconographically, the three-quarter length figure, his pose, and twisting head evoke seventeenth-century works, such as Gregorio Fernández's *Ecce homo* ca. 1625 (Azcoitia, Guipúzcoa).[13] From 1610 onwards, Fernández had carved several celebrated images of the *Ecce homo* and *Christ at the Column*, in which he combined an emotional rendering of the figure with classical restraint to suggest Christ's physical suffering and serene acceptance of his role as sacrificial victim. These works were well-received and quickly established themselves as a prototype for this subject. Perhaps the artist of the Loyola statue had been trained in an earlier manner and now sought to

Cat. 55. (Anderson n. 12373)
Drummer and Dancers. In the late afternoon the drummer walks through the streets beating his drum and playing a pipe to call the dancers to the plaza.

Whereas works depicting Christ's sufferings comprise a significant portion of Holy Week imagery, those depicting the Virgin's pain comprise a more striking presence. The *Mater Dolorosa*, the grieving mother at Christ's Passion, had traditionally appeared in this context, but Spanish art and culture assigned greater prominence to her suffering.[23] The development corresponds to a strong devotion to the Virgin and religious practices that emphasized a Passional Mariology which in turn was linked to the penitential ethos of the confraternities. For many, Christ's death and the Virgin's anguish represented a family tragedy, and the *Mater Dolorosa* became an image one could relate to directly, the grieving mother.

fig. 13
Anonymous Spanish, *Mater Dolorosa*, seventeenth-century (Photo courtesy of The Hispanic Society of America)

Pasos of the Crucifixion, Descent from the Cross, or the Pietà all include dramatic depictions of the Virgin. A seventeenth-century statuette like the anonymous Spanish, *Mater Dolorosa* (Cat. 69: The Hispanic Society of America, D8, fig. 13) reflects the emotional intensity of such works.[24] In particular, it resembles representations of Mary at the foot of the cross, and the piece may well come from a small-scale ensemble depicting the Crucifixion. The figure effectively conveys the Virgin's anguish as she clasps her hands and turns to regard her son. The deeply-cut drapery that flares out around her suggests the speed with which she has moved and enhances the impression of her torment. Depictions of the Crucifixion appear throughout Spain, not only in *pasos* but in all manner of altars and paintings. Given the religious climate and the importance of the moment, this prevalence should not be surprising. Still, as it recalls types found in altars, the Hispanic Society statue points to the transmission of a motif from large-scale projects to those designed for more intimate devotions.

Such worship led to the widespread production of bust-length sculpture of the grieving Virgin like that by José de Mora (Cat. 70: Museo de Arte de Ponce, The Luis A. Ferré Foundation, 66.0574b, fig. 14).[25] These works drew on the viewer's empathy for the Virgin who beholds her son's death. In fact, the figure became a recognized type like the *Ecce homo* and the two were frequently paired in contemporary displays, whether in chapels, sacristies, or convents. Sculptors could heighten the statue's impact in their handling of the Virgin's

fig. 14
José de Mora, *Mater Dolorosa*, ca. 1670-1700? (Photo courtesy of Collection Museo de Arte de Ponce, The Luis A. Ferré Foundation, Inc., Ponce, Puerto Rico)

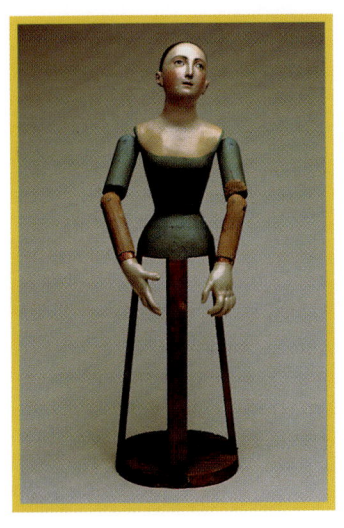

fig. 15 a
Anonymous Spanish, Virgin *(Imagen de vestir: undressed armature of statue)*, ca. 1825
(Photo courtesy of The Hispanic Society of America)

expression, the turn of her body, and the intensity with which she clasped her hands. They also added glass eyes and even glass tears to enhance the effect. Like the *Ecce homo*, some of the most celebrated images of the *Mater Dolorosa* were carved in Granada in the workshops of Pedro de Mena and José de Mora.[26]

The statue from Ponce has been attributed to José de Mora, but it also reveals the interaction between artists as they developed the type according to their own styles. The work probably dates from the outset of Mora's career when he was most susceptible to Mena's example.[27] Mora follows that master's example in carving a bust-length figure with hands held over her heart. Similarly, he recalls Mena's statues in the Virgin's idealized beauty and sorrowing – almost abstracted – gaze which evoke the depths of her grief. The draperies heighten the effect of her pose, particularly the tilt of her head, and her mantle seems to contain her figure so that she appears to retreat into herself, unable to bear the pain. Mora would go on to produce further images of exquisite melancholy and pathos, most notably the *Virgen de las Soledades* (Sta. Ana, Granada). Such statues by both Mora and Mena reflect on a small-scale the intensity of expression found in *pasos* which include depictions of the Virgin's grief.

fig. 15 b
Anonymous Spanish, Virgin *(Imagen de vestir: dressed)*, ca. 1825
(Photo courtesy of The Hispanic Society of America)

The third statue of the Virgin (Cat. 71: The Hispanic Society of America, LD520, fig. 15 a and b) draws attention to another aspect of Marian imagery. This work is an *imagen de vestir*, an image to be clothed; part doll and part statue, these figures consist of a simple wood armature, much like a mannequin, of which only the head and hands would be carved.[28] The figure would then be dressed, and the clothing would hide the structure below while also creating a heightened realistic impression.

Such statues had originated in the sixteenth century and continued into the nineteenth century as seen in the present work which dates ca. 1800-25. The costumes could be elaborate; they were often made from expensive fabrics and might include real jewelry and a crown. The earliest figures wore a white dress with a dark blue mantle to

Notes

Chapter one
SPANISH RELIGIOUS PROCESSIONS:
HOLY WEEK AND CORPUS CHRISTI

1. Muir 1997, pp. 1-8.
2. Loaysa, Biblioteca Colombina mss. 85-5-1, ff. 685-88.
3. For some examples see Casey 1999, p. 40.
4. Casey 1999, pp. 246-47.
5. For a broad discussion of the feast, but with little reference to developments in Spain see Rubin 1991.
6. For surveys discussing the Catholic Reformation see: Koenigsberger 1989, pp. 207-28, and Hsia 1998. Note also Hsia pp. 1-4 for a discussion of historiography.
7. For a comprehensive history see Very 1962. For the drama see Shergold 1967, pp. 52-58, 80-89, and 110-12 and also Stern 1996, pp. 112-24. Lleó Cañal 1975 and 1980 study the festival in Seville. Nalle 1992, pp. 167-69 offers an interesting case study of the holiday's observance in Cuenca.
8. Webster 1998, pp. 151-53.
9. Webster 1998, p. 154.
10. Flynn 1989, pp. 127-28.
11. Payne 1984, p. 50; Christian Jr. 1981, pp. 180-208; Nalle 1992, pp. 149-50.
12. Flynn 1989, pp. 128. For a broader discussion of the implications see Flynn 1989, pp. 128-32.
13. Moreno Navarro, 1986, pp. 39-41 reprints the relevant sections of the synod.
14. Flynn 1989, pp. 129-30 reproduces plates from *Das Trachenbuch des Chirstoph Weiditz von seinem reisen nach Spanien (1529) und den Niederlanden (1531/32)*, Berlin, 1927. The history of the word for this hood, *capirote*, sheds some light on the question. The covered hood was probably first used in processions of mourners to judge by early usage. Among these is the late fifteenth-century manuscript, Juan de Flores, *Triunfo de Amor*, Antonio Gargano ed., Pisa, 1981, p. 132. (I would like to thank John O'Neill of The Hispanic Society of America for the reference from *Dictionary of the Old Spanish Language Project*.) Penitential processions must have turned to the custom as a model fairly early. According to a document of 1586 of the confraternity in the church of Nuestra Señora de la Hiniesta, the word is already in use: José Bermejo y Caballo, *Glorias religiosas de Sevilla o Noticia Histórica-descriptiva de todas las cofradías de Pentiencia y sangre y luz fundadas en esta ciudad*, Seville, 1882, p. 408. Martín Alonso, *Enciclopedia del idioma: Diccionario histórico y moderno de la lengua española (siglo XII al XX) etimología, tecnológico, regional e hispanoamericano*, Madrid, 1958, p. 919 lists the relevant meaning of the word as dating from the seventeenth century. The word clearly had this meaning by 1780 when the Spanish dictionary of the Real Academia explicitly defines *capirote* in this sense.
15. For further contemporary images of penitents see Webster 1998, figs. 5 and 9 (color plate VI).
16. Decree reprinted in Moreno Navarro 1986, p. 40.
17. Webster 1998, pp. 44-45.
18. Brooks 1974, pp. 34-37.
19. Flynn 1989, p. 132.
20. This situation largely holds true today: although women attained the right to march in some processions in the 1980s, they remain a minority. Anecdotes exist, however, of women who inscribe a male relative's name among those marching and then don the penitential costume themselves. Mitchell 1990, pp. 111-12.
21. Garrido Atienza 1889 repr. 1990; Escalera Pérez 1994; and Moreno Cuadro 1997.
22. Garrido Atienza 1889 repr. 1990, pp. 61-64.
23. Lleó Cañal 1980, pp. 44-45.
24. Lleó Cañal 1980, pp. 71-73.
25. Egido 1987, pp. 410-13, 417-18.
26. Palomero Páramo 1987, pp. 50-52.
27. For Valladolid see Agapito y Revilla 1925, pp. 22-26, and for Seville Moreno Navarro 1986, pp. 75-76, 82 and Palomero Páramo 1987, pp. 50-52.
28. Payne 1984, pp. 97-121.

29. Payne 1984, p. 110.
30. González Alcantud, pp. xiv-xv.
31. Moreno Navarro 1986, pp. 75-77, 82-84.
32. Agapito y Revilla 1925, pp. 30-32.
33. Agapito y Revilla 1925, p. 31.
34. For a thorough study of the event and its reporting see Moreno Navarro, 1986, pp. 180-214.
35. Moreno Navarro 1986, p. 213.
36. For detailed and nuanced interpretations of Holy Week in modern Spain see Moreno Navarro 1986 and Mitchell 1990.

Chapter two
ART AND PROCESSIONS IN SPAIN AND THE NEW WORLD

1. Stratton 1993, cat. 47, p. 134.
2. There have been some English-language studies addressing Spanish sculpture: Gómez-Moreno 1931 and 1964, Proske 1951, 1964, and 1967, and more recently Trusted 1995, 1996 and 1997 and Webster 1998. Similarly, apart from the exhibition Stratton 1994, museum visitors in the United States have had few opportunities to see these works.
3. Many of these problems are outlined in Webster 1998, pp. 7-13, and 57-73. Before her, Martín González 1980 had studied the *pasos* of Gregorio Fernández while Brooks 1974 and Trusted 1995 examined the genre of processional sculpture more broadly.
4. St. Teresa of Avila, *The Book of her Life*, vol. 1 in *The Collected Works of St. Teresa of Avila*, trl. K. Kavanaugh O.C.D. and O. Rodriguez O.C.D., Washington, 1976, Chapter 9:1.
5. For an interesting interpretation of this phenomenon with regard to terracottas, *Mater Dolorosas*, and images of St. Francis see Trusted 1997, pp. 46-60.
6. Montoliu 1997, pp. 197-203.
7. Stratton 1994, pp. 155-84.
8. [Proske] 1930, pp. 81-82 and Proske 1951, pp. 270-71. Proske attributes the relief to a woodcarver following the style of Felipe Vigarny (d. 1543), a sculptor active in Burgos and Toledo in the first half of the sixteenth century. A celebrated artist in his lifetime, he entered partnerships with both Alonso Berruguete and Diego de Siloe, and his collaboration with them probably inspired him to include more Italianate and Renaissance elements. With Siloe, Vigarny undertook an important commission of two altarpieces in the Capilla del Condestable, Burgos cathedral. If one accepts Estella Marcos's attributions of their joint work on this project, however, the Hispanic Society relief seems closer to the style of Siloe than Vigarny (Estella Marcos 1995). In this division, the Hispanic Society work resembles, but only in a generalized manner, the reliefs assigned to Siloe (*Visitation* and *Christ at the Column* on the high altar) with regard to the handling of women's profiles and, to a lesser extent, the modeling of Christ. More problematically, the handling of the women's faces and their veils recalls figures carved by Diego de Siloe's father, Gil, in an earlier altar (Sta. Ana, ca. 1500) in the same chapel. To differentiate between Vigarny's and the Siloes' impact on the Hispanic Society relief may be too fine since the work may simply come from the hand of someone who knew the Burgos altarpieces well and may even have formed part of the workshops that produced them. At any rate, the visual comparisons convincingly suggest an origin in Burgos ca. 1525.
9. [Proske] 1930, p. 235; *The Hispanic Society of America Handbook* 1938, pp. 90-91; *A History of The Hispanic Society of America* 1954, pp. 254-55. Proske plausibly relates the figure to processional art, arguing that it perhaps came from a group of Christ Carrying the Cross. She also linked its style to followers of Pedro de Roldán, and this is borne out by comparisons with that artist's St. Roche, ca. 1670-72 (Hospedal de la Caridad, Seville), and the figure of Christ in the

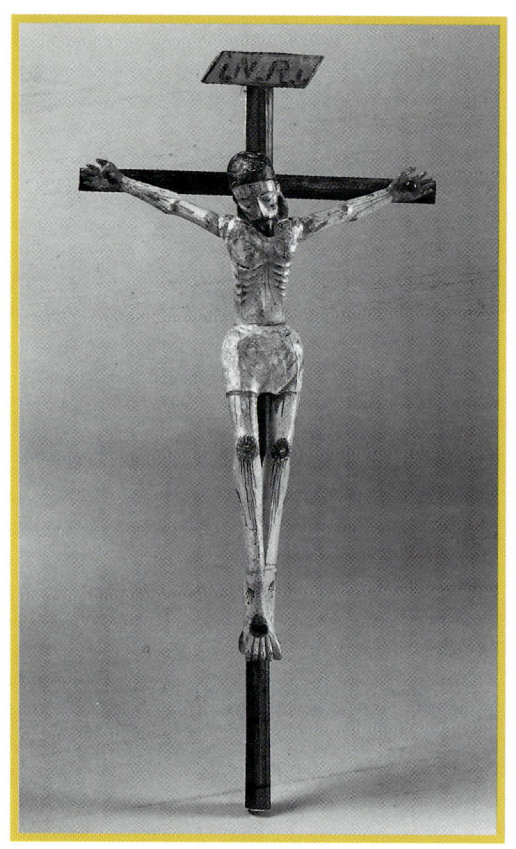

fig. 19
Attributed to the *Santo Niño santero*, *Crucifixion*, ca. 1830,
(Photo courtesy of the Denver Art Museum, Lucile and Donald Graham Collection)

Society of America LA1666, fig. 18) underscores this point. The work depicts a statue venerated in Mexico, but the type had originated in Spain and most Spaniards would immediately have recognized the image of the Virgin holding the Christ Child dressed with crown.[37] Furthermore, the statue functioned much like its counterparts in Europe since it was believed to have miraculous power and was, therefore, taken out in procession to relieve droughts or end plagues.[38] A painting like that by Vásquez tapped into this worship. The artist probably created it for a more personal function – either a small altar in a convent or home – where a local audience who shared this devotion to the *Virgen de los Remedios* could pray to her in private.

Processions in Colonial Latin America might feature widely venerated images, but they also included statues created particularly for the occasion. The most striking of these employ a technique of cornstalk paste that originated in Michoacán (Mexico). In addition to the paste, artists used coral tree, bloom stalk of maguey, maguey fiber, mulberry paper, and orchid bulbs to create lightweight objects, often with a hollow center, that could be carried easily.[39] Using this technique, artists created processional images of the Crucifixion, known as *Cristos de caña*, which emphasize the Savior's suffering: Christ's wounds are vividly rendered with blood running down his body; His head is turned down in complete exhaustion; and His facial features are drawn in an haggard expression of pain.

fig. 20
Pedro Antonio Fresquis, *Crucifixion*, ca. 1790-1831
(Photo courtesy of The Hispanic Society of America)

Statues like these and, more broadly, the entire range of Catholic art which the Spaniards had brought to the New World had a subsequent impact when they inspired a tradition of popular imagery of Christ, the Virgin, and the Saints. The resulting works, known as *santos*, spread Christian imagery yet further. Adding

fig. 21
Pedro Antonio Fresquis, *Virgin of Mt. Carmel*, ca. 1790-1831
(Photo courtesy of The Hispanic Society of America)

folkloric touches, rural artists created paintings and sculptures for devotion on altarpieces in provincial churches and domestic settings. On occasion, the pieces could also be taken out in procession. Stylistically, the works transformed the Spanish images by emphasizing outlines and flat forms to achieve striking emotional and decorative effects. Although developed in Latin America, this tradition entered the United States when the country acquired significant territories from Mexico (including modern day New Mexico) in the settlement of the Mexican War.

How *santeros*, the makers of *santos*, recast the imagery of Christ's Passion and the Virgin's suffering appears in the selection of New Mexican works exhibited. The *Crucifixion*, attributed to the *Santo Niño santero*, ca. 1830, (Cat. 73: Denver Art Museum 1981.123, fig. 19) reflects many *Cristos de caña* in its explicit depiction of Christ's wounds, the streams of blood, and the skin drawn tightly around his ribs. At the same time, the sculptor carves Christ with a tranquil expression and geometric simplicity which confer both folkloric and transcendent qualities on the statue. Similar formal effects can be observed in painting of the *Crucifixion* by Pedro Antonio Fresquis (Cat. 58: The Hispanic Society of America, A8e, fig. 20) which may be only slightly earlier. In his painting, however, Fresquis accentuates the decorative elements of the trees and angels who surround Christ's head and, thus, establishes an effective visual contrast between the figure of Christ and the angels, on the one hand, and the dark background and trees, on the other. The juxtaposition enhances the triumphant note of the iconography. Although Fresquis depicts a wounded Christ dead on the cross, the angels underscore the Savior's divine nature, thereby reassuring the viewer that He will rise.

fig. 22
Rafael Aragón, *Mater Dolorosa*, ca. 1826-65
(Photo courtesy of The Hispanic Society of America)

A comparable delight in patterns and vibrant forms can also be found in four images of the Virgin: Fresquis's *Virgin of Mt. Carmel* (Cat. 59: The Hispanic Society of America, A8b, fig. 21), Rafael Aragón's *Mater Dolorosa* (Cat. 60: The Hispanic Society of America, A8a, fig. 22), and the Quill Pen Master's *Mater Dolorosa* and *Virgin of Guadalupe* (Cat. 61 and 62: The Hispanic Society of America, A8h and A8i, fig. 23 and 24). The *Mater Dolorosa* by the Quill Pen Master (active ca. 1835) and that by Rafael Aragón (active 1826-65) show how *santeros*

39. Luft 1974, pp. 15-26; *Mexico: Splendors of Thirty Centuries* 1990, pp. 264-66; *México en el mundo de las colecciones de Arte: Nueva España* vol. 1, 1994, p. 308.
40. The extent of the images of the Virgin of Guadalupe appears in *Imágenes Guadalupanas: Cuatro siglos*, 1987.
41. For the Virgin of Guadalupe in Mexico see Lafaye 1976.

Chapter three
RUTH ANDERSON: PHOTOGRAPHER OF SPANISH LIFE AND CUSTOMS IN THE 1920S

1. For a more detailed biography of Ruth Anderson see Sider 1998.
2. On the Clarence White School of Photography see Fulton 1996.
3. Alfred Anderson, "Extracts from His Diary," HSA library.
4. Anderson notebooks, 1925-26, Anderson files, Rare Books Department, HSA Library. She drew up this plan prior to her departure for the 1925-26 expedition.
5. The son of a railroad magnate, Archer Huntington rapidly developed a comprehensive interest in Spain's rich culture and traveled extensively throughout the country. After convincing his father of the project's merits, Huntington assembled an impressive collection of rare books and art that would become the nucleus of his projected museum. His plans resulted from long and careful meditation begun early in his youth. He filled his journals and correspondence with musings and notes on the nature such an institution might take, many of which he would subsequently put in to practice.
6. Huntington diary, 1898, HSA Library.
7. Huntington diary, 1898, HSA Library.
8. Archer Huntington, who was particularly dedicated to making Spanish poetry better known in the United States, had the Hispanic Society publish an anthology, *Translations from Hispanic Poets* in 1938. The entire staff of the Society participated in the project, and Ruth Anderson supplied translations of poems by such great Spanish poets as Francisco de Quevedo, Rosalía de Castro, Rubén Darío, Antonio Machado, and Federico García Lorca.
9. Still the day was filled for Alfred Anderson with other reminders of what was absent. They had passed a church "where the choir was practising so I really got to hear some music that sounded like old times, as they were using an ordinary organ." That night on the train, he heard some Spanish boys "softly singing some of their songs, and I began to hum very low to myself some of our dear old Swedish songs." Once they had arrived, he confided "This has been a Christmas day never to be forgotten. Other Christmas days, much happier than this one may be forgotten, but never Christmas day 1924."
10. The train schedules had not always been accommodating; in one instance (April 4, 1925), Ruth Anderson and her father had almost missed the train when they went to the wrong station and could find only a mule and cart to take them to the correct one. They had subsequently hired a French driver, who was paid by the kilometer, and they traveled too slowly for him to earn much: "when we run only a little he appears slightly grief-stricken" (June 8, 1925).

Anderson Photographs and Commentary
ZAMORA
1. Hutton 1906, p. 55.

VILLALCAMPO
1. For photographs of such reenactments see García Rodero 1994, pl. 64-68.

JEREZ DE LOS CABALLEROS
1. For photographs of these figures see García Rodero 1994, pl. 62.
2. For a discussion of confraternities, their rivalries, and their impact on family life in southern Spain see Mitchell 1990, pp. 92-103, and 113-27.

LA ALBERCA
1. Ford 1845, p. 556; Ford 1892, p. 273.
2. Bell 1924, pp. 194-95.

BIBLIOGRAPHY

Agapito y Revilla, Juan. *Las cofradías, las procesiones y los pasos de Semana Santa en Valladolid.* Valladolid, 1925.

Anderson, Janet A. *Pedro de Mena, Seventeenth-Century Spanish Sculptor.* New York, 1998.

Bell, Aubrey F.G. *A Pilgrim in Spain.* Boston, 1924.

Bennassar, Bartolomé. *The Spanish Character: Attitudes and Mentalities from the Sixteenth to the Nineteenth Century.* Trl. Benjamin Keen. Berkeley, Los Angeles, and London, 1979.

Bermejo y Caballo, José. *Glorias religiosas de Sevilla o Noticia Histórica-descriptiva de todas las cofradías de Pentiencia y sangre y luz fundadas en esta ciudad.* Seville, 1882.

Brooks, Joseph C. *The Pasos of Valladolid: A Study in Seventeenth-century Sculpture.* Ph.D. dissertation, University of Chicago, 1974.

Carr, Raymond. *Spain 1808-1975.* Oxford, 1982.

Casey, James. *Early Modern Spain: A Social History.* London and New York, 1999.

Christian Jr., William A. *Local Religion in Sixteenth-Century Spain.* Princeton, 1981.

Clifton, James. *The Body of Christ in the Art of Europe and New Spain: 1150-1800.* Exh. cat. The Museum of Fine Arts, Houston. Munich-New York, 1997.

Díaz-Plaja, Fernando. *La vida española en el siglo XVIII.* Barcelona, 1946.

Domínguez Ortiz, Antonio. "Iglesia institucional y religiosidad popular en la España barroca" in *La fiesta, la cermonia, el rito.* Casa de Velázquez, Universidad de Granada, 1990.

Egido, Teófanes. "La religiosidad de los ilustrados" in *La época de la Ilustración: El estado y la cultura (1759-1808). Historia de España. Tomo XXXI.* Ed. José María Jover Zamora. Madrid, 1987.

Estella Marcos, Margarita. *La imaginería de los retablos de la capilla del Condestable de la catedral de Burgos.* Exh. cat. Burgos Cathedral. n.p., 1995.

Escalera Pérez, Reyes. *La imagen de la sociedad barroca andaluza. Estudio simbólico de las decoraciones efímeras en las fiestas altoandaluzas. Siglo XVII y XVIII.* Málaga, 1994.

Flynn, Maureen. *Sacred Charity. Confraternities and Social Welfare in Spain, 1400-1700.* Ithaca, New York, 1989.

———. "The Spectacle of Suffering in Spanish Streets" in *City and Spectacle in Medieval Europe.* Ed. Barbara A. Hanawalt and Kathryn Reyerson. Minneapolis and London, 1994.

Ford, Richard. *A Handbook for Travellers in Spain and Readers at Home.* London, 1845.

Fulton, Marianne, ed. *Pictorialism into Modernism: the Clarence White School of Photography.* Exh. cat. created by George Eastman House in association with the Detroit Institute of the Arts. New York, 1996.

Gallego y Burín, Antonio. *José de Mora: Su vida y obra.* 1925, reprint Granada, 1988.

fig. 25
Ruth Anderson reading at balcony of fonda: Santa María la Real de Osera, Orense 1925
(Photo courtesy of The Hispanic Society of America)

A S A PERSON, RUTH ANDERSON (1893-1983) REMAINS AN ENIGMATIC FIGURE (fig. 25). Those who knew her at the end of her life recall a determined and formidable woman. At the same time, the few glimpses of her as young woman which her notes reveal suggest another side: a literate sensitivity, a wry humor, and even on occasion uncertainty. In the absence of further information, her biography and the history of the photographs she took for the Hispanic Society must be constructed from other less personal sources.

Born in Nebraska, Ruth Anderson was introduced to photography by her father, Alfred Theodore Anderson, who ran a studio in Kearney specializing in views and portraits.[1] After a year at Nebraska State University (Lincoln), she enrolled at the Nebraska State Teacher's College to become a teacher of history and mathematics. She graduated in 1915 but apparently never worked in any schools. Instead, she reenrolled in Nebraska State University for a semester and then moved to New York City. There she attended the Clarence White School for Photography from which she received a diploma in 1919.

Two years later, she was hired by The Hispanic Society of America where she would work for her entire career, first as a photographer and later as a curator of costume. In this capacity, she made many trips to Spain which furnished her with the images and material for several books.

The training she received from her father and the Clarence White School shaped her approach to photography.[2] Her father accompanied her on one of her earliest trips to Spain, that of 1924-25, offering her the benefit of his experience in field work (fig. 26). At

fig. 26
Alfred Anderson developing photographs in the bathroom of the American Consulate: Vigo, Pontevedra, 1924 (Photo courtesy of The Hispanic Society of America)

Proske, Beatrice Gilman. *Castilian Sculpture. Gothic to Renaissance.* New York, 1951.

———. "Luisa Roldán at Madrid." *The Connoisseur* CLV (1964): 128-32, 199-203, and 269-73.

———. *Martínez Montañés: Sevillian Sculptor.* New York, 1967.

Rubin, Miri. *Corpus Christi: The Eucharist in Late Medieval Culture.* Cambridge, 1991.

Sánchez-Mesa Martín, Domingo. *José Risueño, escultor y pintor granadino, 1665-1732.* Granada, 1972.

———. *El arte del Barroco: Escultura-pintura y artes decorativas. Historia del arte en Andalucía,* vol. 7. Seville, 1989.

Sanz, María Jesús. "Las imágenes vestidas de la Virgen durante el Barroco" in *Pedro de Mena y su Epoca.* Symposium, Junta de Andalucía, 1989, pp. 465-79

Shergold, N.D. *A History of the Spanish Stage from Medieval Times Until the End of the Seventeenth Century.* Oxford, 1967.

Sider, Sandra. "Ruth Matilda Anderson: Biographical Sketchs" in *Ruth Matilda Anderson: Fotografías de Galicia 1924-1926.* Exh. cat. The Hispanic Society of America and Xunta de Galicia, Centro Galego de Artes da Imaxe, 1998.

Stern, Charlotte. *The Medieval Theater in Castile.* Binghamton, New York, 1996.

Stratton, Suzanne L., ed. *Spain, Espagne, Spanien: Foreign Artists Discover Spain 1800-1900.* Exh. cat. The Equitable Gallery in association with The Spanish Institute. New York, 1993.

———. *Spanish Polychrome Sculpture 1500-1800 in United States Collections.* Exh. cat. The Spanish Instutute, Meadows Museum, and Los Angeles County Museum of Art, 1994.

Trusted, Marjorie. "Moving Church Monuments: Processional Images in Spain in the Seventeenth Century." *Journal of the Church Monuments Society* X (1995): 55-69.

———. *Catalogue of the Post-Medieval Spanish Sculpture in Wood, Terracotta, Alabaster, Marble, Stone, Lead and Jet in the Victoria and Albert Museum.* London, 1996

———. "Art for the Masses: Spanish Sculpture in the Sixteenth and Seventeenth Centuries" in *Sculpture and its Reproductions.* Ed. A. Hughes and E. Ranfft, London, 1997, pp. 46-60.

Urrea Fernández, Jesús. *La catedral de Burgos.* Madrid, 1989.

Very, Francis George. *The Spanish Corpus Christi Procession: A Literary and Folkloric Study.* Valencia, 1962.

Webster, Susan Verdi. *Art and Ritual in Golden-Age Spain: Sevillian Confraternities and the Processional Sculpture of Holy Week.* Princeton, 1998.

in 1904 as a "free public library, museum, and educational institution" that would advance the knowledge of Spanish culture. His convictions shaped the approach his museum and its staff would follow. Above all, he resolved that the curators should acquire an intimate firsthand knowledge of their subject, Spain. He had expressed such a belief as early as 1898, when he wrote in his diary:

> *If I ever have a museum, the staff shall know works and* refranes *[Spanish sayings and proverbs] and shall have met native creatures near to men – from mule to bedbug. They shall pursue a word and its feathery meanings as an Englishman seeks the brush of a fox; they must block the burrows of escape and ride off with the trophy. Then they may write about their Spain.*[6]

This is precisely what he did in the 1920s when he sent curators throughout Spain to learn all facets of its art and culture. Moreover, the ethnographic focus of Anderson's campaigns into remote and rural Spain reflects further aspects of Huntington's views. In 1898, after complaining that the average tourist sees only a sentimentalized Spain, he continued:

> *It is in the back country that Spain can be known, in the bare lands that once were covered with great forests and are now inhabited by a scattered and tradition-filled population, one which has preserved the true type better than elsewhere.*
>
> *These amazing peasants, whose struggle for existence is a hard one indeed, are men and women of another age, but fine men and women for all that, erect, preserving an independence and character of truth and honesty which fills one's heart with a sense of freshness and integrity – if you draw near with integrity.*
>
> *I talk with everyone ... From these talks I learn so much more than I can get from many a more instructed friend. Here are the sources of the national values. The blood that runs in these veins is the national blood undiluted by recent contacts with the world outside.*[7]

In pursuit of this authentic Spain, Anderson made four extended expeditions to the country in the 1920s: July 29, 1924-August 28, 1925; November 14, 1925-May 31, 1926; December 29, 1927-April 28, 1928; and October 5, 1929-November 17, 1930. While her father accompanied her on the first, another Hispanic Society photographer, Frances Spaulding, would travel with her subsequently (fig. 29). The last trip, however, also included stops in North Africa, the Azores, and the Canary Islands as well as Portugal. Although she subsequently made one more photographic expedition to Spain (1948-49) as well as several short trips, her most important work dates from the 1920s. Political, economic, and personal considerations had curtailed her visits after 1930. First, the Depression in the United States, then the Spanish Civil War, and finally World War II made travel to Spain difficult. When she could return in the late 1940s, the Hispanic

fig. 29
Frances Spaulding helping to hang a coverlet for photographing: Bendoiro, Lalín, Pontevedra (Photo courtesy of The Hispanic Society of America)

Society was no longer sending curators for such extended stays, and in fact, her trip of 1948-49 marks the last one of such length that any member of the professional staff would take.

While she canvased most parts of Spain, her expeditions focused on the regions of Galicia, Extremadura, and León. The photographs selected for this exhibition come from the last two: Zamora, Villalcampo (province of Zamora), and La Alberca (province of Salamanca) are in León while Jerez de los Caballeros (province of Badajoz) is in Extremadura. Moreover, they offer a representative range of Spain in the 1920s from a provincial capital (Zamora) to a mid-sized town (Jerez de los Caballeros) to villages (Villalcampo and La Alberca). In general, the list of places visited by Anderson in Spain reveals her astute judgment. She had already outlined a thorough process to find images documenting Spanish life and customs – doubtless following directions laid down by Huntington. Nonetheless, learning of such places and photographing them represents a remarkable achievement. Whereas a city like Zamora was well-known and information available in contemporary guidebooks, she could only have learned of events such as the Passion play performed Villalcampo from a local source (fig. 30).

Surprisingly, she made no photographs of Holy Week in Andalusia or Corpus Christi in Toledo, generally acknowledged to be the most famous processions at the time. This absence is puzzling until the conditions under which she worked are recalled. The dates of her trips fell in such a way that she was in Spain for Corpus Christi only in 1925 and 1930. Moreover, Hispanic Society staff were apparently instructed to buy works from local photographers when available. Thus, she purchased a selection documenting these events and refrained from taking many of her own, even though she had witnessed both Holy Week in Seville and Corpus Christi in Toledo (1930). Her program of photography still reflects a bias towards the northwest and west of Spain and a focus on rural rather than urban subjects. Like her shift in style, this may result from Huntington's and the Society's definition of the photographic campaign, which sought

fig. 30
Lunch with our host at the Passion play: Villalcampo, Zamora 1926
(Photo courtesy of The Hispanic Society of America)

out these regions as reflections of a timeless tradition of Castile. Nonetheless, she did not neglect Andalusia but bought a number of photographs for the collection and took many of her own. For instance, at the same time that she let Seville's Holy Week almost pass without photography, she documented the city's subsequent festival, the *feria*, thoroughly.

Her images of religious processions and customs comprise only a part of her work which included all manner of customs. With the passage of time, her interests focused increasingly on costume. Even so, her photography continued to play an important role, by providing her with primary evidence and illustrations for the many books and articles she wrote on the regional dress of Spain. As she did this, the scrupulous notes she had made on these images would prove an invaluable aid. They provide a running commentary on the photographs, frequently including details of the exposure and anecdotes related to their creation. The vignettes she records offer a glimpse of the people featured and suggest just how tenacious and inventive Anderson was as she pursued her goal of documenting Spanish life. Although she never comments explicitly, she had traveled to regions of Spain where life was austere and amenities spartan, even for someone raised in Nebraska in the early twentieth century.

Reading these entries, one cannot help but be impressed at her determination as she experienced such difficult conditions. Occasionally, as in her description of Holy Week in Zamora, a lyrical note creeps into her comments. Such passages remind the reader that in spite of her rigorous scientific approach, she also had a literary side and translated poetry.[8]

A different glimpse into Ruth Anderson's experiences in Spain appears in the diary her father kept of their expedition. He records the difficulties of field work in Spain in a matter of fact tone without complaining. One day the glass lens broke, and they had to use one of the fragments as best they could. Frequently, darkened churches raised difficulties in lighting or required scaffolding for the photograph.

It is slow work photographing in these old churches. The light is usually very dim, and it is hard to focus on anything in the first place. Then the exposures are nearly always very long unless we are photographing only a small area that is not too large for our little flash machine. (January 29, 1925)

In such a church in Pontevedra, the priest allowed Ruth Anderson to play the organ while a fifteen-minute exposure was being shot. After she played "America," he played for Anderson and her father, who subsequently wondered how many of these churches had ever had "America" played in them (letter home of October 6, 1924).

Often the anecdotes of Ruth Anderson's father reveal cordial exchanges with Spaniards who extended them many courtesies, whether providing them with local history or facilitating access to local monuments and their homes. In Santiago, a local author who had helped them, a Sr. Otero, later came to visit them in their hotel. On their departure, Otero gave Ruth Anderson a bouquet which prompted her father to write:

At Tuy the hotel people took us for a wedding couple and wanted to give us the finest room in the house. With the bouquet, I would not have considered it strange if they thought the same here at Santiago. (Letter home of October 6, 1924)

They must have been a distinctive couple: a tall, elegant fifty-nine year old man and a determined, young woman. A local photographer in Santiago took their picture in January and put it in his window. When they returned to the city and saw it, "Ruth did not feel very proud over our appearance on those pictures and she got him to let her have the picture" (May 12, 1925).

Conditions were also not always the most comfortable in hotels. He laments humorously the lack of comfortable chairs, heat in the rooms, and real lights. To remedy the last problem, he simply attached his extension cord to the light and took it where he wanted it or placed it in front of a mirror. Then after describing how he constructed paper shades for the comfort of their eyes, he concludes "we Spanishers have to be resourceful and turn to good use everything that can be used" (April 18, 1925). In a few entries, her father admits, but in a quiet way, to missing his wife and home. On Christmas day both he and Ruth wore a bouquet of daisies "in honor of little mother at home." Otherwise, they spent Christmas like any other day: they photographed a bridge, church, and then a large house outside of Lugo before they caught an evening train to their next destination.[9]

If accommodations offered few luxuries, Ruth Anderson's father had generous praise for the cuisine he sampled: "the Spaniards are not one whit behind the chiefest when it comes to cooking." Both Andersons were attentive to their meals, as he writes "Ruth and I get very well acquainted with the cooks where we stop." By the end of the trip (July 1, 1925), he notes with pride, "I have been down in the kitchen and faced the cook myself and ordered my supper," an achievement for someone whose Spanish was rudimentary. Most entries make some mention to what they ate, and in particular, he singles out quince jelly and *caldo gallego*.

Unfortunately, neither Ruth Anderson nor her companion Francis Spaulding kept a diary of subsequent trips. The photographs they took offer some commentary, however. The most remarkable feature of which is *Nuestra Señora de la Purísima Concepción*, the car they had assembled out of the body of a Fiat, the battery of Chevrolet, and the chassis of a Ford (fig. 31). If Ruth Anderson and her father had cut a striking figure in Spain, Ruth Anderson and Francis Spaulding, two young American women with their car appeared even more so. *Nuestra Señora*, as they called her for short, resolved a serious inconvenience of the previous expedition, transportation.[10]

Thus equipped, Ruth Anderson set off on the subsequent expeditions and photographed the religious processions featured here. Looking at them today, one can only be impressed at the dedication that yielded these images which now seem so much more than "photographic records of the 'ethnographic objects' of Spain."

fig. 31
Ruth M. Anderson beginning to pack the trunk of *Nuestra Señora de la Purísima Concepción*: Val de San Lorenzo, León (Photo courtesy of The Hispanic Society of America)

Anderson

Photographs and Commentary

Zamora

When Ruth Anderson visited Zamora in 1926, it was not just another provincial capital. In particular, it offered a combination of history and tradition that made it especially attractive to someone investigating Spanish life and customs. For the period, it was not a large city: according to the census of 1910, the population numbered 17,163 and in 1920, it had risen only slightly to 17,567. Zamora had played an important role in the Middle Ages, but subsequent history had diminished its national significance. Its cathedral and other churches, ranked among the major Spanish architectural monuments, testify to its past glories. A contemporary guidebook suggests the nostalgia that it could evoke:

> *In the midst of a desert that has blossomed, Zamora stands upon her hill, just a group of golden buildings falling into decay, surrounded by infinite dust and light … The world has forgotten Zamora for many a city less fair, for many a vision less lovely: but few find her out in her ruin and her solitude. Golden and naked she stands on her hill, and only the sun and the wind have loved her these many years.*[1]

Zamora's celebration of Holy Week was then and is still considered among the most notable in Spain, so Anderson's decision to photograph it was a logical part of her program to document the life of Old Castile. The city had recently begun to renovate the festivities, and in the following years, some confraternities would turn to the celebrated sculptor, Mariano Benlliure, for *pasos*. The program of the 1926 celebrations, which Anderson brought back to the Hispanic Society, attests to an extensive series of processions and the broad support they received from the local community including merchants as different as local cafés and a Fiat dealership.

Ruth Anderson photographed events on both Maundy Thursday and Good Friday of 1926. For the purposes of the exhibition, only those of Good Friday, however, have been selected. For Zamora, this day was clearly the most important in the celebration of Holy Week. Once the sequence of *pasos* began, it constituted a sculptural retelling of Christ's passion with floats depicting Christ Bearing the Cross, the Veronica, the *Mater Dolorosa*, Christ Nailed to the Cross and The Raising of the Cross. Anderson's photographs document the masses who witnessed the processions. The images of *pasos* moving through the crowds tellingly suggest their appeal in an urban center. At the same time, the photograph of people gathering in the morning on the outskirts is no less effective, as it evokes the crowd which has assembled preparing to enter the city with the procession. In contrast to the broad, almost impersonal, sweep of these images, other photographs suggest more individualized moments (such as the men preparing to lift up the float). Anderson's interest in costume also led to her record individual penitents. Of these, her image of the brother with his drum presents a forceful image while also documenting one of the most singular aspects of Zamora's Holy Week. Known as the *Merlú*, this drummer and the trumpeter who walks with him play a significant role by indicating the most important moments in the procession with their music.

GOOD FRIDAY APRIL 2, 1926
Good Friday Pasos: *The first procession of* viernes santo *was scheduled to begin at 4:30 A.M. Awakened by hurrying footsteps on the pavement, I went to the window and saw* penitentes *in black carrying black wooden crosses in the dark street. At 6:30 A.M. we joined the crowd.* Pasos *are carried on the shoulders of men. Horizontal bars running from front to back are padded at intervals, a pair of pads for the shoulders of each man. Three pairs across the width of the* paso *and four or five deep, according to size of the* paso. *Holes in the frieze give the outside men a chance to breathe fresh air and to see where they are going. One or two men with their heads wrapped in white kerchiefs direct the movement of the* paso. *The men inside pace in carefully measured steps to avoid treading on each other's heels. The* paso *sways in time to the music played by alternate bands. As it turns a corner, the director seizes hold of the two holes with outstretched hands and shouts directions into the center hole. When the* paso *stops, purple damask hangings are lifted and the men burst forth disheveled to chat with friends or to take a glass of* aguardiente, *their faces flushed, collars open, and kerchiefs all awry. When a* paso *goes under a telegraph wire, the director keeps his hands on the* paso *and focuses his eye on the telegraph wire. The men crouch down and scrape the corner posts of the* paso *(on which it rests when not raised to the men's shoulders) against the ground. "¡Arriba!" The cramped muscles spring at the word and the crucified Christ rises too far. The wire catches on the nail in one hand. The low light of the rising sun glitters on the upcast eye and the sagging mouth of Christ, while the* paso *totters and tosses under the efforts of the men to free the cross from the wire. The Virgin, St. John and the Magdalen preserve their expressions of calm agony but not their equilibrium. The director perspires and shrieks. Two dozen feet shuffle obediently backwards and forwards with knees crouching. The crowd watches intently as the wire slides off the nail a few more inches, another foot forward, and the* paso *is clear, the wire saved. Masculine piety is in evidence today.* Nazarenos *stroll along their black tunics tucked up into a bustle, carrying crosses at all angles, their heads thrown back, puffing cigarettes. The men who are carrying* pasos *swagger about when the procession stops, a hundred Captain Kidds, the knotted kerchief at the head and the swashbuckling air transforms their European clothes into buccaneer's costumes.*

Cat. 1 (Anderson n. 7000)
General view of the crowd and the procession.

Cat. 2 (Anderson n. 7004)
Men receiving encouragement from their friends.
[Editor's note: This photograph shows the structure of the paso's *base as Anderson describes it above, particularly the holes for the men carrying the* paso.*]*

PROCESSION OF GOOD FRIDAY AFTERNOON:
The following series of photographs made from the balcony of the Hotel Suizo overlooking the Plaza Mayor.

Cat. 3. (Anderson n. 7009)
Christ Bearing the Cross.

Cat. 4. (Anderson n. 7010)
Pasos *in crowd:* Verónica, *Christ Bearing the Cross, and* La Virgen de la Soledad.

Cat. 5. (Anderson n. 7011)
La Virgen de la Soledad.

Cat. 6. (Anderson n. 7016)
Nailing Christ to the Cross.

Cat. 7. (Anderson n. 7018)
Raising of the Cross.

Cat. 8. (Anderson n. 7052)
Costume of Penitents. Penitente de la Cofradía de Jesús Nazareno de Penitencia: *full length front robe*, túnica de laval negro; *cowl* capucha, *drum* tambor de ganaderos. Se levantan los pasos al tocar la corneta y el tambor. *He wears also a* decenario con crucifijo *and a cord girdle*, cinturón de esparto.

Villalcampo

Aftter spending Maundy Thursday and Good Friday (April 1 and 2) of 1926 in Zamora, Ruth Anderson traveled into the surrounding countryside to Villalcampo. Here she recorded a procession on Easter Sunday (April 4), another on Easter Monday (April 5), and immediately afterwards, a play reenacting Christ's Passion put on by the villagers. These photographs, but particularly those of the drama, represent some of Anderson's most impressive work. With a recorded population of 971 in 1910 and 922 in 1920, Villalcampo was among the smallest villages that Anderson would visit, although she had been to others that were yet more isolated. Still, the site was remote, and as she herself comments, not many outsiders had ventured there before. The attraction of Villalcampo clearly lay in the play which had not been performed in forty-five years. That she had learned of it is yet another sign of her determination at ferreting out local information which might prove useful to her project.

Notwithstanding the Church's efforts to control religious drama, such reenactments had survived in a handful of remote regions where they continue to this day.[1] Unfortunately, that of Villalcampo is no longer performed, and Anderson's photographs document a tradition now lost. Her desire to record the episode, her interest in costumes, and her sympathy with the actors contribute to the appeal of the pictures she took that day. Her images suggest the enthusiasm of both the country folk in attendance and the villagers who participated. Clearly, Villalcampo commanded modest means, but the earnest efforts of the actors elicited her respect. The stage was a typical wooden structure, hung with modest blankets, doubtless the best backdrop they could afford. The actors' costumes reflect comparable tendencies: St. Peter is dressed rustically, Caiaphas in ecclesiastical attire, and Herod in contemporary military uniform. After viewing the scenes of Christ's Passion and the play's conclusion in which the Virgin holds the dead Christ on her lap, the viewer cannot help but be impressed with the moving and dignified reenactment of the sacred events which Anderson witnessed on April 5, 1926.

EASTER MONDAY APRIL 5, 1926

Passion play – Comedia de la Pasión de Jesús Cristo: libro por autor anónimo. *(I think it was in verse.) The play was last presented forty-five years ago. It is not known when it was first presented. The play was directed by the schoolmaster,* el maestro nacional de Villalcampo, Alcañices, *(Zamora). There were forty-three actors, women and men, and they practiced eight or ten times. They learned to be letter perfect. They had been working about a month and a half.* Se decidió presentar la comedia por espontánea voluntad. Por iniciativa propia con prestación personal universal, se puso el escenario a capricho de la compañía. *They made their own costumes. St. John let his hair grow for the occasion which was a source of great satisfaction to the maestro who regretted that his* Cristo *had not cooperated to the extent of raising a beard.*

People came from a radius of twenty-five kilometers. The priest, the doctor, and his wife seemed to be the only bourgeois in the village. The rest were paisanos. *We were the first foreigners to visit the village.*

On prompters (Anderson n. 6633): The prompter is one of the interesting features of the Spanish Theatre. In Betanzos, he read every word of the play about three beats ahead of the actors and sometimes much louder than they spoke

Preliminary procession through the crowd. Half an hour before the performance began, a herald went about with a bugle announcing the opening of the comedia.

On Roman soldiers (Anderson n. 6640): I tried to find out from what branch of the Spanish army the Roman soldiers had borrowed their suits, but the centurión *refused to come out of his character and insisted that he was a Roman soldier.*

(Anderson n. 6644): The play opened with the firing of a gun by Barrabás, *who then ran away. He was captured by the valiant Roman soldiers and brought back bound with a rope. The play then proceeded with the story of the Passion.*

Cat. 9 (Anderson n. 6629)
The audience on chairs and in trees. The stage was set facing the church.

Cat. 10 (Anderson n. 6631)
The stage, photographed in the morning. The decorations were mainly quilts and blankets, colchas y mantas *of the most vivid hues, yellows and red predominating.*

Cat. 11 (Anderson n. 6635)
The cast: St. Peter, in a dark blue and red colcha, *white wig, and white cap.*

Cat. 12 (Anderson n. 6636)
The cast: Caiaphas in white robe with a cerise chasuble.

Cat. 13 (Anderson n. 6638)
The cast: Herod in a variegated costume, principally red.

Cat. 14 *(Anderson n. 6647)*
The Last Supper.

Cat. 15 *(Anderson n. 6657)*
Flagellation.

Cat. 16 (Anderson n. 6660)
Christ in foreground. Crucifying the bad thief in background. Crosses prostrate.
On the bad thief's costume (Anderson 6665): the costume of the bad thief was a satin, red on one side and yellow on the other.
[Editor's note: The photograph also shows the executioners' brightly colored costumes. This reflects a tradition already present in pasos *from Valladolid where such figures wore the most garish attire.]*

Cat. 17 (Anderson n. 6667)
Christ, the Maries, and St. John.

Cat. 18 (Anderson n. 6670)
Pietà.

Jerez de los Caballeros

RUTH ANDERSON SPENT HOLY WEEK IN 1928 IN JEREZ DE LOS CABALLEROS with the intention of recording its celebrations from Palm Sunday to Good Friday as completely as possible. Although geographically located in the province of Badajoz in Extremadura, the town is not far from Andalusia. Thus it is not surprising that Jerez de los Caballeros (with a population of 10,959 in 1910 and 13,526 in 1920) resembles many small towns of Andalusia. Its processions during Holy Week have enjoyed a modest renown in Spain, and the decision to photograph them again illustrates Anderson's perspicacity. In this case, her choice may also reflect a compromise. Although eager to study customs in Extremadura – she later published a book on the subject – she may have also wanted to include examples of a typical southern Spanish celebration of Easter, but her itinerary and logistics prevented this. Jerez de los Caballeros, therefore, offered her an alternative: a neighboring town where the processions resembled those she could not otherwise see, and one, moreover, located in a region in which she was already interested.

In 1928, the town supported several confraternities, a situation which continues to the present. Just as when Anderson visited, these brotherhoods take pride in their participation during Holy Week, both for the *pasos* they carry in procession and the penitents they muster. Anderson's images thus document rites that still hold great meaning for the residents of Jerez de los Caballeros. At the same time, her photographs suggest how the performance of these rites has evolved. One of the most notable ceremonies Anderson witnessed was the meal for the prisoners which the confraternities brought to the jail on Maundy Thursday and Good Friday. The custom represents a unique variant of the Andalusian practice in which *pasos* are carried by or even brought into the local jail so that the inmates can sing short emotional songs, *saetas*, to the images of Christ or the Virgin. The current practice in Jerez de los Caballeros has, however, changed: now the confraternity of the *Ecce homo*, with support from the municipal government, prepares a *potaje* (stew) at midday for the entire community. In another case, the absence of photographs points to an innovation made after Anderson's visit: since 1984, one confraternity has led a procession on Monday of Holy Week of *empalados*, people carrying crosses which they have tied to their arms. Although Charles III had eliminated such extreme penitence in the eighteenth century, it survives in a neighboring town, Valverde de la Vera (Cáceres).[1] Had, however, the practice been in effect in Jerez de los Caballeros in 1928, Anderson would certainly have recorded it.

Anderson's desire to document the town's observance of Holy Week comprehensively ran up against several difficulties. The streets are narrow and in places admit little light, all of which raised problems of exposure and focus. She chose her positions carefully, however, to deal with these issues while also offering a variety of views of the *pasos* and participants. The images that resulted successfully convey what the different processions were like which, given the field conditions, is no small feat.

In addition to these rites, Anderson took several photographs of the town's residents. These images, notable for their immediacy and presence, enhance the viewer's appreciation of the Holy Week celebrations by adding a personal note. For instance, the photograph, taken on Maundy Thursday, of the men and boys seated on a rooftop vividly evokes the audience's commitment and enthusiasm – they have, after all, clambered up to such precarious seats to view the procession. At the same time, Anderson's judicious framing of the shot strengthens its impact. Similarly, her composition of the photographs of the meal brought to the prisoners heightens the effect. Here she organized the images around the kettles of soup, but as the participants stood before her, she was careful to record their unfeigned sincerity and earnestness. Her portraits of children dressed in the costumes of their confraternities may comprise her most engaging works for the careful seriousness and serene innocence she found in the subjects. These works, however, contain a subtext. The costumes which so interested Anderson serve as an important sign of identity, linking the wearer with a brotherhood. In many Spanish small towns and villages, the identification with a confraternity was crucial since they structured social life by dividing the residents into blocs or factions.[2] To maintain the system, children were taught to relate to their group at an early age, and it is this process which Anderson, perhaps unwittingly, has documented.

ANDERSON NOTES ON JEREZ DE LOS CABALLEROS
PALM SUNDAY: APRIL 1, 1928

Cat. 19. (Anderson n. 9099)
Congregation leaving the church of Santa María. Some of the people carry long cream-colored palm leaves.

Cat. 20. (Anderson n. 9103)
Procession passing through a street. Back view. The maceros *walk on either side of a soldier who carries a banner. Men carry palm leaves.*

Cat. 21. (Anderson n. 9105)

Procession down the Calle Zapatería. Small boys lead the procession carrying a large banner. Another group follows at a distance with a gonfalón bearing the words, Hosanna in excelsis. *Boys dressed in white gowns with long trains, high pointed caps, and long bibs walk on either side of the street. Next comes the* paso *of the Entrance into Jerusalem, called "La burriquita" by the populace. A paso of the Virgin dressed in gorgeous robes and crowned with a large crown and nimbus is accompanied by acolytes and priests.*

Cat. 22. (Anderson n. 9112)
Procession passing through the Plaza. The conductor of the paso *is directing his men to make the turn. The* paso *is the* Entrance into Jerusalem.

Cat. 23. (Anderson n. 9115)
Paso *of the Virgin in the Plaza.*

MAUNDY THURSDAY: APRIL 5, 1928

On Thursday afternoon, the pasos *from the church of San Miguel are carried through the streets. The* pasos *are the* Ecce homo, Oración del huerto, *and* Virgen de la Soledad.

(Anderson n. 9122)
Paso *carriers turning the* Ecce homo.

Cat. 24. (Anderson n. 9125)
Oración del huerto *is preceded by a priest carrying a large* manga.
[In this case manga *refers to a surplice.]*

Cat. 25. (Anderson n. 9128)
Men and boys seated on the coping of a house belonging to the Conde de la Corte.

Comida de los presos *(Anderson n. 9090)*: *The prisoners are given a dinner on Thursday and Friday of Holy Week. Large kettles of soup and basket of bread are carried by boys accompanied by members of the* Cofradía del Ecce Homo. *The brothers of the* Cofradía *wear white tunic with a red cap* (capirote o capirucho) *and a black and white girdle. The banners of the* Cofradía *are carried in the procession which parades through the streets from eleven-thirty to twelve, when it arrives at the prison. The table is set near the door in the prison to receive contributions of money for the dinner.*

Cat. 26. (Anderson n. 9094)
Young men carrying soup kettle: these young men wear wide-trimmed felt hats.

Cat. 27. (Anderson n. 9098)
Row of soup kettles: the kettles are made of copper.

GOOD FRIDAY: APRIL 6, 1928

Cat. 28. (Anderson n. *9130*)
Beginning of Procession. Penitentes *wear white robes and a group of boys carry a banner* gonfalón *of black velvet embroidered in gold,* Hosanna in excelsis.

Cat. 29. (Anderson n. 9132)
Paso: Entry into Jerusalem *from the church of Santa Catalina is carried by the* Cofradía del Rosario, *wearing white tunics and black capes* (gorras) *and bibs. This* paso *is popularly known as* La burriquita.
[Editor's note: The creators of this float went to great lengths to approximate the effect of a live animal: they cured, dried, and stuffed a donkey for the figure of Jesus to ride on.]

[Editor's note: Anderson photographed the next floats in the procession depicting the Last Supper, the Agony in the Garden, Christ Tied to the Column, the Flagellation, Calvary, and an Allegory of Death. Of these, the Agony in the Garden appears in cat. 24 and 32, while the Flagellation is shown in cat. 33.]

Cat. 30. (Anderson n. 9140)
Cristo Yacente: Paso del Señor muerto *from Santa María attended by eight priests and a pair of* Guardia Civil *[sic:* Guardias Civiles*].*
[Editor's note: The glass case of the paso *serves as a coffin-reliquary for the statue of the Dead Christ, and these floats are among the more striking features of Holy Week Processions. During the year, such statues generally remain in this case on an altar to serve as a devotional and Eucharistic image. In one case (Descalzas Reales, Madrid), the image even acts as a repository for the Host.]*

Cat. 31. (Anderson n. 9142)
Paso de la Magdalena *from Santa María. La Magdalena is dressed in a purple robe. Behind her is the* Paso de la Virgen de la Soledad.
[Editor's note: The Virgen de la Soledad *has articulated hands and arms so that she may dry Christ's tears with her handkerchief.]*

Cat. 32. (Anderson n. 9144)
Agony in the Garden.

Cat. 33. (Anderson n. 9146)
El Señor de los Azotes. *The standing figure and the seated figure are called respectively,* Taramilla *and* Zoriaguillo.

Cat. 34. (Anderson n. 9150)
Descent from the Cross.
[Editor's note: This paso *belonging to the Confraternity of* Jesús Nazareno *is no longer used. In 1959, the brothers replaced it with another of the same subject by the sculptor from Huelva, Antonio León Ortega].*

Cat. 35. (Anderson n. 9276)
Child in a penitent costume. The face mask is pinned up on the cap.

Cat. 36. (Anderson n. 9277)
Boy in penitent's costume and another boy. The penitente *wears a white tunic with a long train and purple cap, breast piece and girdle. He accompanied the* Paso de la burriquita *on Palm Sunday afternoon. He carries his train under one arm. The other boy wears a navy blue suit.*

Cat. 37. (Anderson n. 9286)
Small boy with a peaked cap. He wears the maroon costume of the Oración en el huerto. *His peaked cap is tied under his chin.*

La Alberca

From August 15-17, 1930, Ruth Anderson stayed in La Alberca (province of Salamanca). She had come to witness the ceremonies held in honor of the Virgin of the Assumption who was the patroness of the village. They began with a procession of the statue on August 15, the feast of the Assumption, which included a unique ritual, the *ofertorio*. In this, the statue was placed on a temporary altar in the *plaza mayor* so that the parish priest, monks, mayor, town council, and municipal authorities could kneel before the image and pay their respects to it. Moreover, as each one filed before the statue, the village's religious and political hierarchy was manifested. The following day in the same square, two plays were performed in honor of the Virgin; then in the afternoon, a bullfight took place, and the celebrations concluded the next day, the 17th, with a dance in the same square. Combining a religious procession and plays with a bullfight and dance, the festival mingled religious and secular elements effortlessly in a way characteristic of Spanish celebrations. Interestingly, however, this blending no longer occurs: whereas the village continues to hold the procession with *ofertorio* and perform the plays, neither the bullfight nor the dance occurs today.

Like Villalcampo, La Alberca was a small village (with a population of 1,709 in 1910), although unlike the former, it had received some publicity from foreigners, if not always favorable. In 1845, Richard Ford had described it as "dark, dingy, dirty hamlet with prison-like houses, partly built in granite, and wood and plasterwork;" his editors, however, modified the entry in 1892 edition by adding: "its situation is, however, extremely beautiful. The church is worth a visit and contains some curious relics."[1] Aubrey Bell wrote a much more favorable account in 1924, which would almost certainly have caught Anderson's attention for its description of costumes. According to Bell, La Alberca:

> *lies high on the sierra, a beautiful brown village in chestnut trees (somewhat unfairly described by Richard Ford as a "dark, dingy, dirty hamlet") with perhaps 1,500 inhabitants, mostly well-to-do and enterprising peasants. Some of the houses grow out of granite boulders, and women with golden skirts or skirts of orange, gold and brown, wash clothes in the stream below. A wedding or other festival, civil or religious is a wonderfully curious sight. Beautiful ancient plates and old silver are produced for the occasion, friends and neighbours lending their store, and both men and women don their ancient costumes with all their finery of gold and silver. Some of the women daily wear gold earrings and necklaces of beads of gold with small crosses attached: … For special ceremonies all the family heirlooms are worn, nearly all are of gold filagree.*[2]

However Anderson learned of the ceremonies, it was only natural that she should want to photograph them, and again her quest for the authentic Spanish character drew her into remote regions of the country.

The photographs of La Alberca are notable for the way they reflect the variety of this festival. The procession was again difficult to photograph given the dark and narrow streets of the village, but her images effectively suggest the progression of the event. Similarly, the photographs of the plays, the bullfight, and the dance vividly evoke the moment and the enthusiasm of the participants.

ANDERSON NOTES ON LA ALBERCA

FEAST OF THE ASSUMPTION, AUGUST 15-17, 1930

On the feast of the Assumption (Anderson n. 12340): The first day of the fiesta is devoted to religious exercises, and the bullfights are celebrated on the second and third days. El encierro *takes place between six and seven o'clock in the morning of the second day. The cattle men bring the cattle from the ranch, and the youths of the town go out on horseback to meet them and to escort them to the plaza. The youths come in first and gallop across the plaza. Some of their horses are adorned with red saddle cloths and coverings of which six complete sets exist in La Alberca. The plaza is enclosed with wooden stanchions set far enough apart to permit the men to pass between them easily, but close enough to keep out the bull. Three priests stand on the balcony of the town hall at the right. Spectators line the balconies of the houses which overlook the plaza.*

(Anderson n. 12370): The festival of La Alberca is celebrated from the fifteenth to the seventeenth of August. The religious ceremonies are celebrated on the fifteenth and a play is given at the theater in the evening. On the morning of the sixteenth, La Loa *and another drama are played in the open air, and a bullfight is held in the afternoon. If a bull can be persuaded to lend his presence, another bullfight is held on the seventeenth. The young people dance in the plaza in the late afternoon.*

Costumes are worn as follows: 15, día de fiesta religiosa. La gente se pone vestida de honesto o obscuro. 16, día de toros. Por tener muchas preocupaciones no se puede ponerse maja la gente. 17, día de baile. Se pone la gente muy maja.

The pavement of the plaza is very rough and dusty, and the young people would prefer to dance in the pradera *outside the town. The mothers and fathers, however, like to have their sons and daughters under their eyes, and will consent to letting them dance only once a year at Easter time in the grassy meadow.*

LA ALBERCA, AUGUST 15, 1930
Procession and homage to the Virgin

Cat. 38. (Anderson n. 12418)
Image of the Virgin entering the plaza. The image of the Virgin is mounted on a platform andas *under a canopy* (arco) *which rests on four posts* (postes). *The* andas *is of gilded wood* madera dorada. *Four men carry the shafts* palos *in front and back and two assist at the sides. The men are dressed in long capes of black woollen stuff. Four civil guards carrying their hats accompany the image.*
On the image of the Niño Jesús (Anderson n.12417): The image is set on a platform under an arch of artificial flowers, is carried by four men wearing cotton blouses. The image is being set on a stand on the opposite side of the plaza from where the image of the Virgin is to be placed.

Cat. 39. (Anderson n. 12423)

Image of the Virgin crossing the plaza. The image is sharply tilted as it is lowered into place. Two priests in dalmatics and one in a cope face the image.

[Editor's note: Anderson also photographed the Salutation of the priests. (Anderson n. 12427-28): three priests salute the Virgin and then seat themselves on a bench at her left.]

The image of the Virgin (Anderson n. 12409): it will be placed on a stand at one side of the plaza *in front of the* La Escuela de Niños. *The stand consists of old chestnut tables covered with cloths.*

Cat. 40. (Anderson n. 12430)
Salutations of the monks. The monks kneel several times as they approach the Virgin. After their salutation they take their places beside the priests. It is not recorded that the priests and monks made any offering. [Editor's note: Anderson also photographed the Ofertorio de la Justicia.
(Anderson n. 12431): The dignitaries of the Justicia *which comprises the* alcalde, *the* juez, *eight* concejales, *the* fiscal *and the* superante *[?] make the first offering. They form themselves into two files and advance in pairs toward the Virgin. The mayor and the judge precede the rest. They offer silver from one to five pesetas each. The dignitaries are dressed in long capes of black woollen material.]*

Cat. 41. (Anderson n. 12435)
Ofertorio de las mayordomas. *There are six* mayordomas *dressed in black lace* mantillas. *They give a silver reliquary and lace trimmed* escarapeliz *[sic:* escarapela*] for a priest.*

Cat. 42. (Anderson n. 12426)
Image of the Virgin leaving the plaza. Back View. When the ceremonies of the offertories are completed, the image of the Virgin is carried from the plaza through a corner opposite to that by which it was brought in. The Virgin is preceded by the Niño Jesús.

Cat. 43. (Anderson n. 12444)
Image of the Virgin leaving the plaza. The women follow the Virgin. They wear over their heads kerchiefs, lace mantillas *of black satin and velvet.*

Procesión del Rosario *(Anderson n. 12442): After vespers the image of the Virgin is carried through the streets. At the head of the procession are two acolytes* (monaguillos) *dressed in red woollen robes with rochets of white linen. The acolytes carry processional candle holders* (ciriales) *of silver with lighted candles. The street is the* Calle del Tablado.

Cat. 44. (Anderson n. 12445)

Procesión del Rosario *approaching the church. The standard of the Virgin (Anderson n. 12443): it is of blue and white satin embroidered with gold and adorned with gold fringe. The standard is carried by one of the* mayordomos *of whom there are eight, four* entrantes *and four* salientes. *They carry staffs* (cetros) *of wood upon which is mounted a device* (escudo) *of silver.*

Cat. 45. (Anderson n. 12451)
Procesión del Rosario. *Image of the Virgin. The Virgin wears a white mantle embroidered in gold. The crown of gold is set with precious stones. About the wrists are pieces* manillos ? *of white satin embroidered with gold and set with precious stones. Rings and other jewelry are also of gold. The* Virgen de la Asunción *is the* patrona *of the town.*

Cat. 46. (Anderson n. 12448)
Procesión del Rosario. *Image of the Virgin entering the church.*

AUGUST 16, 1930 PLAY

The stage consists of a rough platform of planks built to face the porch of the parish church. A long curtain of red and white cotton print hangs from tall poles in front of the stage and shorter curtains of vari-colored prints form the "backdrop." A street opening behind the platform gives the actors access to the stage without passing in front of the audience. A high awning made of sacking partially cuts off the August sun from the spectators who are seated in chairs and benches on the pavement in front of the stage. Each householder has brought or sent his own chair or bench. The mayor of the town and other dignitaries sit comfortably in the shade of the porch of the church.

Cat. 47. (Anderson n. 12381)
The prompter's box is indicated by the arched rod which is placed at the center front of the stage. A cloth will be spread over this rod to conceal the prompter from the audience. A guardia civil *stands beside the back curtain at the left.*

Drama La Loa *Scene 1 (Anderson n. 12391): The scene is laid in Madrid. A* serrano *of La Alberca is talking to a* señorito, *who was also born in La Alberca. The* serrano *is trying to persuade the* señorito *who is ill and weary of life in Madrid, to return to La Alberca for the festival of the Virgin and to remain in the Sierra....*
Drama La Loa *Scene 2 (Anderson n. 12392): Devil on the* serpiente. *The devil is seated upon a device (*serpiente) *which represents the seven deadly sins. The device is mounted at the top of a slide made of planks. To the six arms at the front of the device are fixed fireworks which will be exploded as the devil and the* serpiente *descend the slide. The prompter projects out of his box.*

Cat. 48. (Anderson n. 12393)
Drama La Loa *Scene 2. Several men support the* serpiente *as it descends down the slide. The prompter has withdrawn out of his box.*

Cat. 49. (Anderson n. 12394)
Drama La Loa *Scene 2. Explosion of the* serpiente. *A chair and an umbrella have been raised for protection against the explosion.*

The devil (Anderson n. 12396): he makes a defiant speech against the forces of good. He wears a cap of black velvet. The cap is also called a kind of pasamontaña. *The doublet?* (jubón o jugón) *also of black velvet is made with a triangular breast piece* (pechera o peto) *long, pointed sleeves and gathered skirt* (faldilla). *The breast piece and sleeves caps are red and the fringe on the skirt is gold. The breeches are of black velvet and the stockings and shoes are black.*

Drama La Loa *Scene 3. Two monks on their way to the Fiesta. A Franciscan and a Carmelite, natives of La Alberca, meet a* cabrero *of Sequeros on their way to the* fiesta. *The devil overtakes them and after some argument, he attacks them and throws them upon the ground.*

Cat. 50. (Anderson n. 12400)
Drama La Loa *Scene 3. The Devil overthrowing the monks. The Archangel Michael is about to appear.*

The devil is about to carry them off to hell, when the Archangel Michael appears and saves them. The devil is vanquished and the monks and the goatherd swear devotion to the Virgin. The Loa *is played annually at the fiesta.*

Cat. 51. (Anderson n. 12401)
Drama La Loa *Scene 3. Archangel Michael banishing the Devil. The Archangel Michael is represented by a girl wearing a dress of white silk and wings made of cardboard and adorned with painted cloth* (tela pintada). *She wears necklaces of gold on which are hung Spanish doubloons* (onzas) *of the sixteenth ? century.*

Cat. 52. (Anderson n. 12364)
Bullfighter capeando. *Seats for spectators (Anderson n. 12344):* Heavy planks are suspended with ropes from the beams which support the balconies of the houses facing the Plaza Mayor. *The planks are high enough to be out of the reach of the bull's horns. Ladders will be placed against the columns to enable the spectators to reach their seats.*

Cat. 53. (Anderson n. 12370)
The jota *(Anderson n. 12376): it is most frequently danced. The two-step and the fox trot are frowned upon in La Alberca, for the parents do not approve of the young people dancing* agarrados.

Cat. 54. (Anderson n. 12372)
File of dancers. The young men and women dance in opposite files. Sometimes girls dance together. Young men may "cut in" as often as they like.

Cat. 55. (Anderson n. 12373)
Drummer and Dancers. In the late afternoon the drummer walks through the streets beating his drum and playing a pipe to call the dancers to the plaza.

Checklist

PAINTINGS

Cat. 56
Philip Villamil (British, active 1838-70)
"Los Nazarenos": The Penitents' Procession, Seville, ca. 1860
Oil on canvas, 142.2 x 114.3 cm.
The Hispanic Society of America, LA1074

Cat. 57
José María Vásquez (Mexican, active 1793-1827)
Virgen de los Remedios, 1826
Oil on canvas, 62.2 x 48.3 cm.
The Hispanic Society of America, LA1666

Cat. 58
Pedro Antonio Fresquis (New Mexican, 1749-1831)
Crucifixion, ca. 1790-1831
Oil or water-based media on wood, 53.8 x 34 cm.
The Hispanic Society of America, A8e

Cat. 59
Pedro Antonio Fresquis (New Mexican, 1749-1831)
Virgin of Mt. Carmel, ca. 1790-1831
Oil or water-based media on wood, 35.7 x 20.2 cm.
The Hispanic Society of America, A8b

Cat. 60
Rafael Aragón (New Mexican, active 1826-65)
Mater Dolorosa
Oil or water-based media on wood, 29.3 x 17.8 cm.
The Hispanic Society of America, A8a

Cat. 61
Quill Pen Master (New Mexican, active ca. 1835)
Mater Dolorosa
Oil or water-based media on wood (pine)
26.6 x 17.7 cm.
The Hispanic Society of America, A8h

Cat. 62
Quill Pen Master (New Mexican, active ca. 1835)
Virgin of Guadalupe
Oil or water-based media on wood, 32.5 x 21.6 cm.
The Hispanic Society of America, A8i

SCULPTURE

Cat. 63
Anonymous Castilian
The Deposition, ca. 1525
Polychromed wood (walnut) with *estofado*
80 x 75.9 cm.
The Hispanic Society of America, D14

Cat. 64
Anonymous Andalusian
Simon of Cyrene [?], ca. 1675-1700
Polychromed wood, 32.9 cm.
The Hispanic Society of America, D31

Cat. 65
Anonymous Andalusian
Saint Joseph [?], ca. 1725-50
Polychromed wood with *estofado*, 40.7 cm.
The Hispanic Society of America, D6

Cat. 66
Anonymous Castilian
Ecce homo, ca. 1600
Polychromed wood with gilding, beads of glass,
36.8 cm. (without base)
The Martin D'Arcy Museum of Art, Loyola
University Chicago, 16.81

Cat. 67 (not in exhibition)
Attributed to José de Risueño (1665-1732)
and Workshop
Ecce homo, ca. 1712-32
Polychromed wood, 69.9 cm.
Yale University Art Gallery, Stephen Carlton Clark,
B.A. 1903, Fund, 1964.52

Cat. 68
Circle of Juan de Juni
Christ Carrying the Cross, ca. 1545
Polychromed wood, 32.8 x 20.4 cm.
The Hispanic Society of America, D25

Cat. 69
Anonymous Spanish
Mater Dolorosa, seventeenth century
Polychromed wood with *estofado*, 33.5 cm.
The Hispanic Society of America, D8

Cat. 70 (not in exhibition)
José de Mora (Spanish, 1642- 1724)
Mater Dolorosa, ca. 1670-1700
Polychromed wood with silver gilding,
glass eyes, 52.4 cm.
Collection Museo de Arte de Ponce, The Luis A.
Ferré Foundation, Inc., Ponce, Puerto Rico,
66.0574b.

Cat. 71
Anonymous Spanish
Virgin, ca. 1825
Polychromed wood, textile, 54 cm.
The Hispanic Society of America, LD520

Cat. 72
Francisco de Ribas (Spanish, 1617-1679)
Blessing Christ Child, ca. 1645
Polychromed wood, 80 cm. (with pedestal)
The Hispanic Society of America, LD1720

Cat. 73
Attributed to the *Santo Niño santero*
(New Mexican)
Crucifixion, ca. 1830
Polychromed wood, 69.9 x 35.6 cm.
Denver Art Museum, Lucile and
Donald Graham Collection, 1981.123

METALWORK
Cat. 74
Anonymous Spanish
Crucifix, seventeenth century
Gilded bronze, 26.9 cm.
The Hispanic Society of America, R3020

Cat. 75
Anonymous Zacatecas Silversmith
Monstrance, 1770-1800
Silver-gilt, 90 cm.
The Hispanic Society of America, R3032

Notes

Chapter one
SPANISH RELIGIOUS PROCESSIONS:
HOLY WEEK AND CORPUS CHRISTI

1. Muir 1997, pp. 1-8.
2. Loaysa, Biblioteca Colombina mss. 85-5-1, ff. 685-88.
3. For some examples see Casey 1999, p. 40.
4. Casey 1999, pp. 246-47.
5. For a broad discussion of the feast, but with little reference to developments in Spain see Rubin 1991.
6. For surveys discussing the Catholic Reformation see: Koenigsberger 1989, pp. 207-28, and Hsia 1998. Note also Hsia pp. 1-4 for a discussion of historiography.
7. For a comprehensive history see Very 1962. For the drama see Shergold 1967, pp. 52-58, 80-89, and 110-12 and also Stern 1996, pp. 112-24. Lleó Cañal 1975 and 1980 study the festival in Seville. Nalle 1992, pp. 167-69 offers an interesting case study of the holiday's observance in Cuenca.
8. Webster 1998, pp. 151-53.
9. Webster 1998, p. 154.
10. Flynn 1989, pp. 127-28.
11. Payne 1984, p. 50; Christian Jr. 1981, pp. 180-208; Nalle 1992, pp. 149-50.
12. Flynn 1989, p. 128. For a broader discussion of the implications see Flynn 1989, pp. 128-32.
13. Moreno Navarro, 1986, pp. 39-41 reprints the relevant sections of the synod.
14. Flynn 1989, pp. 129-30 reproduces plates from *Das Trachenbuch des Chirstoph Weiditz von seinem reisen nach Spanien (1529) und den Niederlanden (1531/32)*, Berlin, 1927. The history of the word for this hood, *capirote*, sheds some light on the question. The covered hood was probably first used in processions of mourners to judge by early usage. Among these is the late fifteenth-century manuscript, Juan de Flores, *Triunfo de Amor*, Antonio Gargano ed., Pisa, 1981, p. 132. (I would like to thank John O'Neill of The Hispanic Society of America for the reference from *Dictionary of the Old Spanish Language Project*.) Penitential processions must have turned to the custom as a model fairly early. According to a document of 1586 of the confraternity in the church of Nuestra Señora de la Hiniesta, the word is already in use: José Bermejo y Caballo, *Glorias religiosas de Sevilla o Noticia Histórica-descriptiva de todas las cofradías de Pentiencia y sangre y luz fundadas en esta ciudad*, Seville, 1882, p. 408. Martín Alonso, *Enciclopedia del idioma: Diccionario histórico y moderno de la lengua española (siglo XII al XX) etimología, tecnológico, regional e hispanoamericano*, Madrid, 1958, p. 919 lists the relevant meaning of the word as dating from the seventeenth century. The word clearly had this meaning by 1780 when the Spanish dictionary of the Real Academia explicitly defines *capirote* in this sense.
15. For further contemporary images of penitents see Webster 1998, figs. 5 and 9 (color plate VI).
16. Decree reprinted in Moreno Navarro 1986, p. 40.
17. Webster 1998, pp. 44-45.
18. Brooks 1974, pp. 34-37.
19. Flynn 1989, p. 132.
20. This situation largely holds true today: although women attained the right to march in some processions in the 1980s, they remain a minority. Anecdotes exist, however, of women who inscribe a male relative's name among those marching and then don the penitential costume themselves. Mitchell 1990, pp. 111-12.
21. Garrido Atienza 1889 repr. 1990; Escalera Pérez 1994; and Moreno Cuadro 1997.
22. Garrido Atienza 1889 repr. 1990, pp. 61-64.
23. Lleó Cañal 1980, pp. 44-45.
24. Lleó Cañal 1980, pp. 71-73.
25. Egido 1987, pp. 410-13, 417-18.
26. Palomero Páramo 1987, pp. 50-52.
27. For Valladolid see Agapito y Revilla 1925, pp. 22-26, and for Seville Moreno Navarro 1986, pp. 75-76, 82 and Palomero Páramo 1987, pp. 50-52.
28. Payne 1984, pp. 97-121.

29. Payne 1984, p. 110.
30. González Alcantud, pp. xiv-xv.
31. Moreno Navarro 1986, pp. 75-77, 82-84.
32. Agapito y Revilla 1925, pp. 30-32.
33. Agapito y Revilla 1925, p. 31.
34. For a thorough study of the event and its reporting see Moreno Navarro, 1986, pp. 180-214.
35. Moreno Navarro 1986, p. 213.
36. For detailed and nuanced interpretations of Holy Week in modern Spain see Moreno Navarro 1986 and Mitchell 1990.

Chapter two
ART AND PROCESSIONS IN SPAIN AND THE NEW WORLD

1. Stratton 1993, cat. 47, p. 134.
2. There have been some English-language studies addressing Spanish sculpture: Gómez-Moreno 1931 and 1964, Proske 1951, 1964, and 1967, and more recently Trusted 1995, 1996 and 1997 and Webster 1998. Similarly, apart from the exhibition Stratton 1994, museum visitors in the United States have had few opportunities to see these works.
3. Many of these problems are outlined in Webster 1998, pp. 7-13, and 57-73. Before her, Martín González 1980 had studied the *pasos* of Gregorio Fernández while Brooks 1974 and Trusted 1995 examined the genre of processional sculpture more broadly.
4. St. Teresa of Avila, *The Book of her Life*, vol. 1 in *The Collected Works of St. Teresa of Avila*, trl. K. Kavanaugh O.C.D. and O. Rodriguez O.C.D., Washington, 1976, Chapter 9:1.
5. For an interesting interpretation of this phenomenon with regard to terracottas, *Mater Dolorosas*, and images of St. Francis see Trusted 1997, pp. 46-60.
6. Montoliu 1997, pp. 197-203.
7. Stratton 1994, pp. 155-84.
8. [Proske] 1930, pp. 81-82 and Proske 1951, pp. 270-71. Proske attributes the relief to a woodcarver following the style of Felipe Vigarny (d. 1543), a sculptor active in Burgos and Toledo in the first half of the sixteenth century. A celebrated artist in his lifetime, he entered partnerships with both Alonso Berruguete and Diego de Siloe, and his collaboration with them probably inspired him to include more Italianate and Renaissance elements. With Siloe, Vigarny undertook an important commission of two altarpieces in the Capilla del Condestable, Burgos cathedral. If one accepts Estella Marcos's attributions of their joint work on this project, however, the Hispanic Society relief seems closer to the style of Siloe than Vigarny (Estella Marcos 1995). In this division, the Hispanic Society work resembles, but only in a generalized manner, the reliefs assigned to Siloe (*Visitation* and *Christ at the Column* on the high altar) with regard to the handling of women's profiles and, to a lesser extent, the modeling of Christ. More problematically, the handling of the women's faces and their veils recalls figures carved by Diego de Siloe's father, Gil, in an earlier altar (Sta. Ana, ca. 1500) in the same chapel. To differentiate between Vigarny's and the Siloes' impact on the Hispanic Society relief may be too fine since the work may simply come from the hand of someone who knew the Burgos altarpieces well and may even have formed part of the workshops that produced them. At any rate, the visual comparisons convincingly suggest an origin in Burgos ca. 1525.
9. [Proske] 1930, p. 235; *The Hispanic Society of America Handbook* 1938, pp. 90-91; *A History of The Hispanic Society of America* 1954, pp. 254-55. Proske plausibly relates the figure to processional art, arguing that it perhaps came from a group of Christ Carrying the Cross. She also linked its style to followers of Pedro de Roldán, and this is borne out by comparisons with that artist's St. Roche, ca. 1670-72 (Hospedal de la Caridad, Seville), and the figure of Christ in the

Descent from the Cross, ca. 1670-72 (Hospedal de la Caridad, Seville).

10. [Proske] 1930, p. 257; *The Hispanic Society of America Handbook* 1938 p. 92; *A History of The Hispanic Society of America* 1954, p. 335. Proske published the statue as Portuguese on the basis of a pencil inscription on the base, which reads "Convent of Lowas, Coimbra." Proske assumed that the inscription should be read as the Convent of Loios, Coimbra. Unfortunately, I have found no information on the existance of such a convent. No provenance information is available prior to its purchase (date unknown in the United States). Stylistically, the figure suggests an eigtheenth-century sculptor from Andalusia, perhaps one familiar with the types established by the Mora workshop in Granada. At present, the statue cannot be attributed any more closely because comparisons point out only general similarities. The handling of the head on the Hispanic Society piece recalls a tradition that begins with José de Mora's *St. Joseph* ca. 1712, (Cartuja, Granada see Gallego y Burín 1925 repr. 1988, p. 188) and continues with Risueño's *St. Joseph* 1712-32 (Museo de Bellas Artes, Granada see Sánchez-Mesa Martín 1972, cat. 74) and Agustín de Vera Moreno's *St. Joseph* ca. 1748, (N. Sra. de las Angustias, Granada see Sánchez-Mesa Martín 1989, p. 278). The flowing draperies of the Hispanic Society most closely resemble another work in Granada, the series of apostles, 1714-17 (N. Sra. de las Angustias, Granada see Sánchez-Mesa Martín 1989, pp. 259-61) carved by Pedro Duque de Cornejo (1678-1757). The polychromy – combining an extensive use of gilding and punchwork over which the artist has painted – presents no ready comparisons with documented pieces of these masters. In fact, the technique seems remarkably dissimilar from most examples.
11. Moreno Navarro 1986, pp. 99-107.
12. Stratton 1994, cat. 31, p. 141 gives the date as eighteenth century, but this seems implausible. Although the piece entered the museum dated to the early seventeenth century, it was subsequently reassigned to the eighteenth century on the basis of comparisons to the Granadine school of the Moras and their followers. Such claims are not totally convincing given the differences in figure type, realization of the head, facial expresson, and the *estofado* technique. Moreover the base is admittedly ca. 1600, and it would be odd, but not impossible, to put a later statue on an earlier base.
13. Martín González 1980, pp. 175-76.
14. The sculptor may also have enhanced this effect by adding a crown of thorns and rope to bind Christ's hands.
15. Stratton 1994, cat. 21, p. 121; Clifton 1997, cat. 34, p. 80. The date for the Yale piece follows that established by Sánchez-Mesa Martín for the comparable *Ecce homo* in Granada: Sánchez-Mesa Martín 1972, cat. 38. See below note 18.
16. For examples that show how pervasive the theme was in the seventeenth century see Sánchez-Mesa Martín 1989, pp. 91, 101, 115, 229, 231, and 252.
17. See *Pedro de Mena y Castilla* 1989; Anderson 1998; and Gallego y Burín 1925, repr. 1988.
18. For a history of the *Ecce homo* in the Capilla Real, Granada and its attribution see Sánchez-Mesa Martín 1972, cat. 37, pp. 187-89. The attribution is accepted by Martín González 1983, pp. 424-25. The most notable attribution prior to this occurred in Gallego y Burín 1925, repr. 1988, pp. 168-70.
19. [Proske] 1930, p. 123; *The Hispanic Society of America Handbook* 1938, p. 83 relates to the followers of Juni working in Sahagún near León ca. 1545.
20. For *Cristo de los huevos* and its history in the Burgos Cathedral see López Mata 1950 and Urrea Fernández 1989. The desire to replicate a statue like the *Cristo de los huevos* also reflects its local prominence. The statue had entered Burgos in the fifteenth century and found its way into the Cathedral in 1836. As its origins were mysterious, it acquired a miraculous provenance: allegedly carved by Joseph of Arimathea and subsequently passed to Syria. It came to Spain when a Burgalese merchant found it miraculously floating in a box at sea during a storm. Its miracles continued on entering the city when it several times rejected efforts to move it from its chapel or refused a crown of gold offered as a donation.
21. Webster 1998, pp. 65-67 discusses such descent ceremonies in Seville.

22. The interpretation of the egg included in another work, Piero della Francesca's Brera Altarpiece (Brera, Milan), has generated significant bibliography addressing the meaning of such a symbol. See Millard Meiss, "*Ovum Struthionis*: Symbol and Allusion in Piero della Francesca's Montefeltro Altarpiece" in Millard Meiss, *The Painter's Choice: Problems in the Interpretation of Renaissance Art*, New York, 1976, pp. 105-29 and Ronald Lightbown, *Piero della Francesca*, New York, London, and Paris, 1992, pp. 252-53.
23. Mitchell 1990, pp. 164-80.
24. [Proske] 1930, p. 237; *A History of The Hispanic Society of America* 1954, p. 298.
25. Stratton 1994, cat. 28, p. 135.
26. For statues by Mena of the *Mater Dolorosa* see Anderson 1998, cat. 21-27; Sánchez-Mesa Martín 1989, pp. 220-30; *Pedro de Mena y Castilla* 1989, cat. 7, 9, 11, and 13; and Orueta y Duarte 1914, pp. 154, 171, 175, 185, 186, 203, 211, 226, 248, 252, and 262. For those by José de Mora see Gallego y Burín 1925, repr. 1988, pp. 149-72.
27. The intertwining of type and hand already makes individual attributions difficult, but this case points out further complexities in Granadine sculpture: the collaboration that existed at various times between members of the Mena and Mora families. Bernardo de Mora (1614-84), the head of that family, had studied with Alonso de Mena (1587-1646) and subsequently married a sister of his master. On Alonso's death, Bernardo entered into a partnership of sorts with Alonso's son, Pedro de Mena. Pedro de Mena doubtless influenced Bernardo, but after more than a decade, Pedro transferred his workshop to Málaga in 1658. Meanwhile, Bernardo continued in Granada where he collaborated with his son, José, on occasion. In 1685, moreover, José had married a cousin of his on the Mena side, thereby continuing the relation between the two families.
28. For these images and their history see Webster 1998, pp. 59-65; Martínez-Burgos García 1989, pp. 149-59; Sanz 1989, pp. 465-479; *Pequeñas imágenes de la pasión en Valladolid*, 1987.
29. Sanz 1989, pp. 467, 471.
30. Sanz 1989, p. 472.
31. Martínez-Burgos García 1989, pp. 150-54; *Pequeñas imágenes de la pasión en Valladolid* 1987, cat. 38 and 44-51.
32. García Rodero 1994, pl. 86 and p. 280.
33. Maldonado Dávila Saavedra, Seville: Biblioteca Colombina mss. 84-7-20, f.172v.
34. For a catalogue and history of these objects see Hernmarck 1987.
35. *The Hispanic Society of America Handbook* 1938, p. 204 publishes the work as Spanish. An almost identical piece, however, has been subsequently discovered bearing the mark of Zacatecas, Mexico, but it unfortunately does not include the silversmith's mark. See *La orfebrería hispanoamericana en Andalucía occidental* 1995, cat. 36, p. 94.
36. For the statue and the function of such imagery in Seville see Lenaghan 2000, pp. 46-54.
37. Among the many books written on the statue, several also included prints of the image, thereby further testifying to its appeal. These works, like the Hispanic Society painting, also strengthened the veneration of the statue by making it better known. I am grateful to Mitchell Codding for these references: Francisco de Florencia, *La milagrosa invención de un tesoro escondido en un campo que hallò un cazique,* [Mexico], 1685; Ignacio Carrillo y Pérez, *Lo máximo en lo mínimo, la portentosa imágen de Nuestra Señora de los Remedios, Conquistadora y Patrona de la imperial ciudad de Mexico*, Mexico, 1808; *Consejos espirituales, dados por un religioso a una alma deseosa de unirse con Dios*, Mexico, 1819. In adddition, a print of 1759 is illustrated in Fray Francisco de Ajofrín, *Diario del viaje que por orden de la Sagrada Congregación de Propaganda Fide hizo a la América Septentrional en el siglo XVIII*, Archivo documental español publicado por la Real Academia de la Historia, XII, ed. Vicente Castañeda y Alcover, Madrid, 1958, p. 113.
38. The painting's inscription reads: "La milagrosicima imagen de Nra Sra DE LOS REMEDIOS que se venera en su santuario extra muros de Mejico. Es el remedio de todas las calamidades de dicha ciudad, desuerte que en la escasés de lluvias, Peste, y otras necesidades, la condusen en una solemne Prosećión para la Santa Yglesia Catedra, y en su noven[ario] se experimenta grandes prodigios."

39. Luft 1974, pp. 15-26; *Mexico: Splendors of Thirty Centuries* 1990, pp. 264-66; *México en el mundo de las colecciones de Arte: Nueva España* vol. 1, 1994, p. 308.
40. The extent of the images of the Virgin of Guadalupe appears in *Imágenes Guadalupanas: Cuatro siglos*, 1987.
41. For the Virgin of Guadalupe in Mexico see Lafaye 1976.

Chapter three
RUTH ANDERSON:
PHOTOGRAPHER OF SPANISH LIFE
AND CUSTOMS IN THE 1920S

1. For a more detailed biography of Ruth Anderson see Sider 1998.
2. On the Clarence White School of Photography see Fulton 1996.
3. Alfred Anderson, "Extracts from His Diary," HSA library.
4. Anderson notebooks, 1925-26, Anderson files, Rare Books Department, HSA Library. She drew up this plan prior to her departure for the 1925-26 expedition.
5. The son of a railroad magnate, Archer Huntington rapidly developed a comprehensive interest in Spain's rich culture and traveled extensively throughout the country. After convincing his father of the project's merits, Huntington assembled an impressive collection of rare books and art that would become the nucleus of his projected museum. His plans resulted from long and careful meditation begun early in his youth. He filled his journals and correspondence with musings and notes on the nature such an institution might take, many of which he would subsequently put in to practice.
6. Huntington diary, 1898, HSA Library.
7. Huntington diary, 1898, HSA Library.
8. Archer Huntington, who was particularly dedicated to making Spanish poetry better known in the United States, had the Hispanic Society publish an anthology, *Translations from Hispanic Poets* in 1938. The entire staff of the Society participated in the project, and Ruth Anderson supplied translations of poems by such great Spanish poets as Francisco de Quevedo, Rosalía de Castro, Rubén Darío, Antonio Machado, and Federico García Lorca.
9. Still the day was filled for Alfred Anderson with other reminders of what was absent. They had passed a church "where the choir was practising so I really got to hear some music that sounded like old times, as they were using an ordinary organ." That night on the train, he heard some Spanish boys "softly singing some of their songs, and I began to hum very low to myself some of our dear old Swedish songs." Once they had arrived, he confided "This has been a Christmas day never to be forgotten. Other Christmas days, much happier than this one may be forgotten, but never Christmas day 1924."
10. The train schedules had not always been accommodating; in one instance (April 4, 1925), Ruth Anderson and her father had almost missed the train when they went to the wrong station and could find only a mule and cart to take them to the correct one. They had subsequently hired a French driver, who was paid by the kilometer, and they traveled too slowly for him to earn much: "when we run only a little he appears slightly grief-stricken" (June 8, 1925).

Anderson Photographs and Commentary
ZAMORA
1. Hutton 1906, p. 55.

VILLALCAMPO
1. For photographs of such reenactments see García Rodero 1994, pl. 64-68.

JEREZ DE LOS CABALLEROS
1. For photographs of these figures see García Rodero 1994, pl. 62.
2. For a discussion of confraternities, their rivalries, and their impact on family life in southern Spain see Mitchell 1990, pp. 92-103, and 113-27.

LA ALBERCA
1. Ford 1845, p. 556; Ford 1892, p. 273.
2. Bell 1924, pp. 194-95.

Bibliography

Agapito y Revilla, Juan. *Las cofradías, las procesiones y los pasos de Semana Santa en Valladolid.* Valladolid, 1925.

Anderson, Janet A. *Pedro de Mena, Seventeenth-Century Spanish Sculptor.* New York, 1998.

Bell, Aubrey F.G. *A Pilgrim in Spain.* Boston, 1924.

Bennassar, Bartolomé. *The Spanish Character: Attitudes and Mentalities from the Sixteenth to the Nineteenth Century.* Trl. Benjamin Keen. Berkeley, Los Angeles, and London, 1979.

Bermejo y Caballo, José. *Glorias religiosas de Sevilla o Noticia Histórica-descriptiva de todas las cofradías de Pentiencia y sangre y luz fundadas en esta ciudad.* Seville, 1882.

Brooks, Joseph C. *The Pasos of Valladolid: A Study in Seventeenth-century Sculpture.* Ph.D. dissertation, University of Chicago, 1974.

Carr, Raymond. *Spain 1808-1975.* Oxford, 1982.

Casey, James. *Early Modern Spain: A Social History.* London and New York, 1999.

Christian Jr., William A. *Local Religion in Sixteenth-Century Spain.* Princeton, 1981.

Clifton, James. *The Body of Christ in the Art of Europe and New Spain: 1150-1800.* Exh. cat. The Museum of Fine Arts, Houston. Munich-New York, 1997.

Díaz-Plaja, Fernando. *La vida española en el siglo XVIII.* Barcelona, 1946.

Domínguez Ortiz, Antonio. "Iglesia institucional y religiosidad popular en la España barroca" in *La fiesta, la cermonia, el rito.* Casa de Velázquez, Universidad de Granada, 1990.

Egido, Teófanes. "La religiosidad de los ilustrados" in *La época de la Ilustración: El estado y la cultura (1759-1808). Historia de España. Tomo XXXI.* Ed. José María Jover Zamora. Madrid, 1987.

Estella Marcos, Margarita. *La imaginería de los retablos de la capilla del Condestable de la catedral de Burgos.* Exh. cat. Burgos Cathedral. n.p., 1995.

Escalera Pérez, Reyes. *La imagen de la sociedad barroca andaluza. Estudio simbólico de las decoraciones efímeras en las fiestas altoandaluzas. Siglo XVII y XVIII.* Málaga, 1994.

Flynn, Maureen. *Sacred Charity. Confraternities and Social Welfare in Spain, 1400-1700.* Ithaca, New York, 1989.

———. "The Spectacle of Suffering in Spanish Streets" in *City and Spectacle in Medieval Europe.* Ed. Barbara A. Hanawalt and Kathryn Reyerson. Minneapolis and London, 1994.

Ford, Richard. *A Handbook for Travellers in Spain and Readers at Home.* London, 1845.

Fulton, Marianne, ed. *Pictorialism into Modernism: the Clarence White School of Photography.* Exh. cat. created by George Eastman House in association with the Detroit Institute of the Arts. New York, 1996.

Gallego y Burín, Antonio. *José de Mora: Su vida y obra.* 1925, reprint Granada, 1988.

García Rodero, Cristina. *Festivals and Rituals of Spain*. J.M. Caballero Bonald (text), New York, 1994.

Garrido Atienza, Manuel. *Antiguallas Granadinas. Las fiestas del Corpus*. 1889. Reprint, with introduction by José Antonio González Alcantud, Granada, 1990.

———. *Las fiestas de la toma*. 1892. Reprint, with introduction by José Antonio González Alcantud, Granada, 1998.

Gómez-Moreno, Manuel. *Renaissance Sculpture in Spain*. Trl. Bernard Bevan. Florence, 1931.

———. *The Golden Age of Spanish Sculpture*. Notes on the plates by María Elena Gómez-Moreno. New York, 1964.

González Alcantud, José Antonio. Introduction to Manuel Garrido Atienza, *Las fiestas de la toma*. 1892. Reprint, Granada, 1998.

———. Introduction to Manuel Garrido Atienza, *Antiguallas Granadinas. Las fiestas del Corpus*. 1889. Reprint, Granada, 1990.

Hernández Díaz, José. *Juan de Mesa*. Seville 1983.

———. *Juan Martínez Montañés (1568-1649)*. Seville, 1987.

Hernmarck, Carl. *Custodias procesionales en España*. Madrid, 1987.

The Hispanic Society of America Handbook: Museum and Library Collections. New York, 1938.

A History of The Hispanic Society of America: Museum and Library 1904-1954. New York, 1954.

Hsia, R. Po-Chia. *The World of Catholic Renewal: 1540-1770*. Cambridge, 1998.

Hutton, Edward. *The Cities of Spain*. New York, 1906.

Imágenes Guadalupanas: Cuatro siglos. Exh. cat. Centro Cultural/ Arte Contemporáneo. Mexico, 1987.

Koenigsberger, H.G., George L. Mosse, and G.Q. Bowler. *Europe in the Sixteenth Century*. Second ed. London and New York, 1989.

Lafaye, Jacques. *Quetzalcóatl and Guadalupe: The Formation of Mexican National Consciousness 1531-1813*. Trl. Benjamin Keen. Chicago and London, 1976.

Lenaghan, Patrick. "Artists and Markets in Seventeenth-Century Seville: Francisco de Ribas's *Blessing Christ Child* at The Hispanic Society of America." *The Sculpture Journal* IV (2000): 46-54.

Lleó Cañal, Vicente. *Arte y espectáculo. La fiesta del Corpus Christi en Sevilla en los siglos XVI y XVII*. Seville, 1975.

———. *Fiesta Grande: El Corpus Christi en la historia de Sevilla*. Seville, 1980.

Loaysa, Juan de. *Memorias Sepulchrales de esta Santa Iglesia Patriarchal de Sevilla en Epitaphios, Capillas, Entierros*. Seville: Biblioteca Colombina mss. 85-5-1. [Second copy: 84-7-35]

López Mata, Teófilo. *La catedral de Burgos*. Burgos, 1950.

Luft, Enrique. "Las imágenes de caña de maíz de Michoacán." *Artes de México* XIX (1974): 15-27.

Maldonado Dávila Saavedra, Joseph. *Discurso Historico de la Real Capilla de Sevilla,* in *Memorias que tocan a la Santa Iglesia Metropolitana y Patriarchal de Sevilla y Fundaciones de algunos monasterios de dicha ciudad.* Seville: Biblioteca Colombina mss. 84-7-20.

Martín González, Juan José. *El escultor Gregorio Fernández.* Madrid, 1980.

———. *Escultura barroca en España.* Madrid, 1983.

Martínez-Burgos García, Palma. "Las imágenes de vestir: El origen de una devoción barroca" in *Pedro de Mena y su Epoca.* Symposium, Junta de Andalucía, 1989, pp. 149-59

México en el mundo de las colecciones de Arte: Nueva España: vol. 1. Mexico, 1994.

Mexico: Splendors of Thirty Centuries. Exh. cat. The Metropolitan Museum of Art. New York, 1990.

Mitchell, Timothy. *Passional Culture: Emotion, Religion, and Society in Southern Spain.* Philadelphia, 1990.

Montoliu, Violeta. *Mariano Benlliure (1862-1947).* Valencia, 1997.

Moreno Cuadro, Fernando. *Arte efímero andaluz.* Cordoba, 1997.

Moreno Navarro, Isidoro. *La Semana Santa de Sevilla: Conformación, mixtificación y significación.* Second ed. Seville, 1986.

———. "Niveles de significación de los íconos religiosos y rituales de reproducción de identidad en Andalucía" in *La fiesta, la ceremonia, el rito.* Casa de Velázquez, Universidad de Granada, 1990.

Muir, Edward. *Ritual in Early Modern Europe.* Cambridge, 1997.

Nalle, Sarah T. *God in La Mancha: Religious Reform and the People of Cuenca 1500-1650.* Baltimore and London, 1992.

La orfebrería hispanoamericana en Andalucía occidental. Exh cat. Fundación El Monte. Seville, 1995.

Orueta y Duarte, Ricardo de. *Pedro de Mena.* Madrid, 1914.

Palomero Páramo, Jesús Miguel. *La imaginería procesional sevillana: misterios, nazarenos y cristos.* Second ed. Seville, 1987.

Payne, Stanley G. *Spanish Catholicism: An Historical Overview.* Madison, 1984.

Pedro de Mena y Castilla. Exh. cat. Valladolid, Museo Nacional de Escultura. Valladolid, 1989.

Pequeñas imágenes de la pasión en Valladolid. Exh. cat. Valladolid, Museo Nacional de Escultura. Valladolid, 1987.

[Proske], Beatrice Gilman. *Catalogue of Sculpture (Sixteenth to Eighteenth Centuries).* New York, 1930.

Proske, Beatrice Gilman. *Castilian Sculpture. Gothic to Renaissance.* New York, 1951.

———. "Luisa Roldán at Madrid." *The Connoisseur* CLV (1964): 128-32, 199-203, and 269-73.

———. *Martínez Montañés: Sevillian Sculptor.* New York, 1967.

Rubin, Miri. *Corpus Christi: The Eucharist in Late Medieval Culture.* Cambridge, 1991.

Sánchez-Mesa Martín, Domingo. *José Risueño, escultor y pintor granadino, 1665-1732.* Granada, 1972.

———. *El arte del Barroco: Escultura-pintura y artes decorativas. Historia del arte en Andalucía,* vol. 7. Seville, 1989.

Sanz, María Jesús. "Las imágenes vestidas de la Virgen durante el Barroco" in *Pedro de Mena y su Epoca.* Symposium, Junta de Andalucía, 1989, pp. 465-79

Shergold, N.D. *A History of the Spanish Stage from Medieval Times Until the End of the Seventeenth Century.* Oxford, 1967.

Sider, Sandra. "Ruth Matilda Anderson: Biographical Sketchs" in *Ruth Matilda Anderson: Fotografías de Galicia 1924-1926.* Exh. cat. The Hispanic Society of America and Xunta de Galicia, Centro Galego de Artes da Imaxe, 1998.

Stern, Charlotte. *The Medieval Theater in Castile.* Binghamton, New York, 1996.

Stratton, Suzanne L., ed. *Spain, Espagne, Spanien: Foreign Artists Discover Spain 1800-1900.* Exh. cat. The Equitable Gallery in association with The Spanish Institute. New York, 1993.

———. *Spanish Polychrome Sculpture 1500-1800 in United States Collections.* Exh. cat. The Spanish Instutute, Meadows Museum, and Los Angeles County Museum of Art, 1994.

Trusted, Marjorie. "Moving Church Monuments: Processional Images in Spain in the Seventeenth Century." *Journal of the Church Monuments Society* X (1995): 55-69.

———. *Catalogue of the Post-Medieval Spanish Sculpture in Wood, Terracotta, Alabaster, Marble, Stone, Lead and Jet in the Victoria and Albert Museum.* London, 1996

———. "Art for the Masses: Spanish Sculpture in the Sixteenth and Seventeenth Centuries" in *Sculpture and its Reproductions.* Ed. A. Hughes and E. Ranfft, London, 1997, pp. 46-60.

Urrea Fernández, Jesús. *La catedral de Burgos.* Madrid, 1989.

Very, Francis George. *The Spanish Corpus Christi Procession: A Literary and Folkloric Study.* Valencia, 1962.

Webster, Susan Verdi. *Art and Ritual in Golden-Age Spain: Sevillian Confraternities and the Processional Sculpture of Holy Week.* Princeton, 1998.